Alice Farnham is a renowned
BBC Radio 4's Woman's Hour *M....*
Today's Ten Best Women Conductors. She has conducted orchestras,
opera and ballet companies worldwide including the BBC Concert
Orchestra, Royal Scottish National Orchestra, National
Symphony Orchestra of Ireland, the Royal Opera House, Welsh
National Opera, Mariinsky Theatre, Calgary Opera, Opéra de
Rouen, and Folkoperan Stockholm. She is founder and Artistic
Director of Women Conductors with the Royal Philharmonic
Society, the National Concert Hall Female Conductor Programme
in Dublin, and Perth Symphony Orchestra's Women on the Podium
– giving hundreds of women the chance to further their prospects
and find their calling as conductors. She trained with the legendary
conducting pedagogue Ilya Musin in St Petersburg, and was
an Organ Scholar at St Hugh's College, Oxford University. She
was shortlisted for the 2024 Royal Philharmonic Society
Conductor Award.

Further praise for *In Good Hands*:

'Explores the process of conducting, demystifying the work while
leaving magic intact.' Terri Apter, *Times Literary Supplement* Books
of the Year

In Good Hands

The Making *of a* Modern Conductor

Alice Farnham

faber

First published in 2023
by Faber & Faber Ltd
The Bindery, 51 Hatton Garden
London, ECIN 8HN

This paperback edition first published in 2024

Typeset by Faber & Faber Ltd
Printed in the UK by CPI Group (UK) Ltd, Croydon, CRO 4YY

A CIP record for this book
is available from the British Library

ISBN 978–0–571–37051–1

10 9 8 7 6 5 4 3 2 1

Dedicated to the loving memory
of Graham Garton

Contents

Conductors Interviewed   ix

Introduction   1

Part I

1 The Start   17
2 The Basics: Hands and Baton   30
3 Lighting the Fire   42
4 Preparation to Performance   60
5 Training   88
6 Careers   126

Part II

7 Opera   151
8 Ballet   195
9 New Music   222
10 Reaching Out   237

Part III

11 We Need to Talk about Breasts   259

Coda   284
Acknowledgements   287
Index   291

Conductors Interviewed

Marin Alsop
American conductor; Chief Conductor, Vienna Radio Symphony Orchestra; Artistic Director & Chief Conductor, Polish Radio Symphony Orchestra; Principal Conductor, London Philharmonia Orchestra; former Principal Conductor, Bournemouth Symphony Orchestra; former Music Conductor, São Paulo Symphony Orchestra.

Richard Baker
British composer and conductor, specialising in contemporary music. Guest conducting includes London Sinfonietta, Birmingham Contemporary Music Group, and Royal Opera House.

Kalena Bovell
Panamanian-American conductor, poet and advocate; former Assistant Conductor, Memphis Symphony Orchestra; Conductor, Memphis Youth Symphony.

Olivia Clarke
British-Irish conductor; Charles Mackerras Conducting Fellow, English National Opera; Assistant Conductor, City of Birmingham Symphony Orchestra.

In Good Hands

Laurence Cummings
British harpsichordist and conductor; Muisc Director, The
Academy of Ancient Music; William Crotch Professor,
Royal Academy of Music.

Sian Edwards
British conductor; Professor and Head of Conducting,
Royal Academy of Music; Professor of Conducting,
University of Music and the Performing Arts, Vienna;
former Music Director, English National Opera.

Ben Glassberg
British conductor; Music Director, Volksoper Wien; Music
Director, Opéra de Rouen Normandie.

Jane Glover
British conductor and musicologist; Music Director,
Chicago's Music of the Baroque; former Music Director,
the London Mozart Players.

Helen Harrison
British conductor; Music Director, Young Sinfonia (Royal
Northern Sinfonia's youth orchestra), Blackpool Symphony
Orchestra, Preston Opera.

Jonathon Heyward
African-American conductor; Chief Conductor,

Nordwestdeutsche Philharmonie; Music Director,
Baltimore Symphony Orchestra.

Tianyi Lu
Chinese-New Zealand conductor; Conductor-in-Residence,
Stavanger Symphony Orchestra; former Female Conductor-
in-Residence, Welsh National Opera; former Assistant
Conductor, Los Angeles Symphony Orchestra, Melbourne
Symphony Orchestra.

Eímear Noone
Irish conductor and composer; best known for award-
winning work on video and gaming music.

Antonio Pappano
Italian-British-American conductor and pianist; Music
Director elect, London Symphony Orchestra; Music
Director, The Royal Opera, London.

Maria Seletskaja
Estonian conductor, former professional ballet dancer;
Music Director, English National Ballet.

Bramwell Tovey
British conductor and composer; Principal Conductor,
BBC Concert Orchestra; former Music Director, Vancouver
Symphony Orchestra. *In memoriam.*

In Good Hands

Barry Wordsworth
British conductor; Principal Guest Conductor, former Music Director, The Royal Ballet, London; Conductor Laureate, BBC Concert Orchestra.

All biographies correct at time of publication.

Introduction

It was 26 September 2019, and I was conducting Mozart's 'Paris' Symphony to a happily noisy audience – applauding, cheering and generally making appreciative sounds while we performed. Sometimes they were excitedly shushing each other so they could hear a quiet section; sometimes there was a magical hush until the next surprise loud moment.

Was this a children's concert perhaps, or an unusual venue such as a shopping centre, or were we simply providing background music? There's a time and a place for that important work, but no, this was an evening with the BBC Concert Orchestra at the Queen Elizabeth Hall on London's Southbank. Is this normal for a classical concert? In Mozart's time it certainly was, but it is so alien to a modern audience that not only did we have to give permission to the audience to behave in this way but we also had to workshop the idea with them at the start, forcing them to let their hair down.

It was one of the most artistically, and musically satisfying concerts I have ever conducted. Although we were playing on modern instruments rather than the subtly different instruments Mozart would have written for, we played it with a decent respect for Mozart's style, rehearsing and performing with careful attention to detail. The BBCCO is a wonderfully versatile orchestra and the rehearsal process had gone well, once I reassured them that the authentic re-enactment we were attempting didn't require them to wear wigs and tights. It was the authentic sound of the *audience* that most interested us.

The environment of a classical concert can be off-putting – a bit like going to a church service and not knowing when to stand or sit. There is a whole set of expected behaviours that can leave the uninitiated feeling unwelcome. It's hardly a relaxing environment conducive to listening properly. How do we break down these barriers and make the concert hall a more welcoming environment for people of all ages and backgrounds? Perhaps by looking at how things used to be done? This was the brainchild of broadcaster and presenter Tom Service, who suggested Mozart's 'Paris' Symphony was the perfect piece to start unapologetically breaking today's rules. In Mozart's letters to his father, he described at great length how enthusiastically the audience responded on first hearing this symphony. If Mozart visited earth today and heard performances of his music, he'd assume from our silence throughout that we just didn't like it.

There is a relatively recent rule in classical music that applause between movements of a work is forbidden. Concert halls and orchestras rarely insist on this; rather it is something that has evolved over the centuries and comes mostly from audiences rather than from performers. It makes no difference how a movement ends. Some movements fade to an atmospheric silence before emerging into the next movement, and then perhaps applause seems insensitive.

Another movement might culminate in a cascading fountain of sound that surely cries out for applause. Unless it is the final movement of the work, it is most definitely frowned on to applaud, though you are permitted to clear your throat, because apparently a smattering of ugly coughs is an acceptable noise to make. The same mostly unspoken rule applies all over the world of the classical concert. Pity the poor soul who enthusiastically applauds at the triumphant end of the third movement of Tchaikovsky's Sixth Symphony! Do they not know that there's another movement to come? In some places they might even get shushed by their neighbours, but they should certainly feel deeply embarrassed and ashamed. It is only in the concert hall where this happens. In ballet, audiences frequently applaud when they see something they love on stage. Just so in opera: at the end of a spectacular aria the audience (much to the chagrin of some stage directors) can burst into spontaneous applause, regardless of what's happening in the drama. In jazz, it would be downright rude not to clap after a solo and in church, it's perfectly acceptable for the organ music at the start and end of a service to be accompanied by a bit of chat. Can you imagine an audience at Glastonbury sitting still and silent?

So, Tom and I talked to the audience at the start. We gave them permission to listen and make noise, just the way Mozart had described it. He had written two second (slow) movements, so we played an excerpt of each and let the audience choose, by way of a clapometer, which was to be performed. As far as we could tell, both options were equally popular, and interestingly there had been a similar 50–50 opinion when we had asked the orchestra earlier in the day, so I made the casting vote. Sometimes conductors have their uses. Between movements the audience was not only permitted to applaud, but we encouraged them to chat about what they thought of the music so far to their neighbour, even if they'd never met before. The orchestra talked too, and I stepped off the podium for a few friendly words with the leader.

The programme, entitled *Orchestra Unwrapped*, was an exploration of what makes a modern symphony orchestra. The second half comprised works by living composers, two of whom (Dobrinka Tabakova and Graham Fitkin) were in attendance. There was film music, TV theme tunes, and more traditional works from the twentieth century. Tom interviewed me, the composers and the leader of the orchestra. The audience played its part too, and the spontaneous response to the music continued into the second half – gasps of fear at the high strings in *Psycho*, nervous laughter at *Jaws*, even clapping along to the BBC *Animal Magic/W1A* theme tune. There was respectful attentive silence at the start of Elgar's 'Nimrod', then a cheer when it reached its culmination. Many of the players said afterwards the whole experience made them less nervous, they felt the audience was with them, a living organism they could bounce off, rather than the usual wall – the silent critical mass. I felt that too. A conductor has their back to the audience, so it's particularly hard to pick up an atmosphere until the end, but not that evening.

I am sure there were some who felt it was distracting and annoying, and I can understand that, but I challenge anyone who says it's dumbing down. The audience was engaged and listening, and it made for an interesting Radio 3 *Afternoon Concert* when it was broadcast a few months later. There are times when I love more than anything the stillness of an audience that allows me to disappear into the music. But I have no doubt there is space for both experiences in the concert hall, not just as an experiment, but as a mainstream way of performing classical music.

The next day I was back in the opera world, with some of the country's most talented young singers at the Guild-hall School of Music & Drama. The production was Haydn's comic opera *La fedeltà premiata* – a ridiculously complicated story even by operatic standards, which the director Stephen Barlow was cleverly shaping into refined but thoroughly enjoyable entertainment. My job as conductor was to work alongside him, to guide, support and lead these singers, the student music staff, and later in the process the student orchestra. The fact that they were students made very little difference to our approach and expectations. As with most students at conservatoire level, they were already performing to a high professional standard. These opera productions are a consolidation of years of training, and open to a paying public, with invited agents and promoters; they are reviewed in the national press. But the rehearsal process for the students is also important, and this is where my job is most interesting. I love the opera rehearsal period, so it is a particularly happy part of my work. I enjoy making music with young performers. You're unlikely to come across a cynical or jaded music student, and their enthusiasm is infectious.

We rehearsed from 10 a.m. to 5 p.m. from Monday to Friday. Quite civilised office hours one might think, but for all involved in the production our work continues outside the rehearsal room – preparation time for each rehearsal, and students must fit lessons around the schedule.

I was busy on three consecutive weekends that October – teaching conductors' workshops for women in Oxford, London and Dublin respectively. Just over five years before, I had decided to shake up the world of conducting by simply encouraging women to consider it. In 2014, if you googled 'orchestral conductor', a picture of a conductor-shaped balloon appeared before that of a female conductor. That same year, according to Christina Scharff's report *Equality and Diversity in the Classical Music Profession*, the gender ratio of conductors holding titled conducting positions (music director, principal conductor, assistant conductor, etc.) with professional UK orchestras was a toe-curling 1.4 per cent.* I knew the only way to tackle this was by taking positive action at grass-root level. It was a simple, almost naive idea, but it was working, and the climate was rapidly changing for the good. I believed I was the right person to lead this revolution in the UK because I had broken through

---

* See also Christina Scharff, *Gender, Subjectivity and Cultural Work: The Classical Music Profession* (London: Routledge, 2017).

debilitating inhibitions and insecurities to enjoy successes that were unimaginable to my teenage self. I knew there were plenty of women out there with the qualities to become a conductor and all they needed was the right encouragement. I knew how to enable the talented but underconfident to tap into their natural communication skills, to trust their musical instincts and training, and to own that space on the podium. Starting at Morley College, I found a new home for the Women Conductors programme at the Royal Philharmonic Society in 2016 and it has been thriving ever since.

The first weekend was exactly thirty years after I had started my undergraduate years at Oxford University as a very confused young woman, amazed at the confidence of my peers, and utterly convinced that I didn't deserve to be there. On this Saturday morning, I walked into a quiet and tense room containing twelve very serious women. With these workshops, some people are completely new to conducting, others are quite experienced, and it works particularly well when the level of musicianship is high. After three hours, with the help of two professional pianists and the body language coach Alma Sheehan, the participants were laughing and partaking in the playful yet serious work of communicating music. By the end of the first day, as they prepared to meet a small string ensemble, far from becoming more nervous, they were ready and willing. The next day a carefully selected group of professional string players, most of whom had worked with me many times before, allowed this safe space and positive learning environment to continue.

The aim is that by the end of the workshop every participant feels at least more confident to stand in front of people and wave. Some might decide that conducting is probably not for them, or think they might come back to it later, but a small group will be determined to take it further as soon as they possibly can. By 2019 I had worked with nearly five hundred women – and not just in the UK. So, by 2019, there were already women forging ahead in advanced conducting training and early careers.

The following weekend I was teaching alongside Sian Edwards, Head of Conducting at the Royal Academy of Music, and a long-time hero of mine. She was helping develop this wave of emerging female conductors by running short courses preparing women to apply for postgraduate study, giving them that extra push and an equity they needed to reach the next level.

One more workshop weekend, this time at the National Concert Hall in Dublin, with a similar group to the Oxford course. I was to work with this new cohort of conductors for a year – or as it turned out much longer, as we struggled with Covid lockdowns to complete the programme by early 2022. By late October 2019 I was running on empty and had given myself a bad cold. After an inspiring but exhausting first day, I took some Night Nurse, went to bed early, and twelve hours later woke up in a panic realising I had slept through my alarm. Luckily the hotel was opposite the NCH, and I got there with minutes to spare. I took a flight back to London that evening, then up early for rehearsals of the opera. This had been ticking along nicely all the way through this period, and we were moving into the final stages of rehearsal.

I rarely work in one place for longer than a few months, so over the years I have discovered an excellent way of feeling rooted in my place of work. When I arrive somewhere new, I will seek out the cafe with the nicest ambience serving the best coffee and croissants. Then for that period of work, be it two weeks or two months, I shall try to go there every day. My aim is that by the end of the first week we greet each other by name, and they start making my coffee (double-shot Americano with hot milk on the side) before I put in my order. There's a cafe in Stockholm where they remembered after a six-month absence. That morning, back in London, I poured the contents of a Lemsip Max sachet into a 'keep cup' and asked the barista for some hot water, but she misheard my croaks and made my usual double-shot Americano. It was just about drinkable when I thought of it as coffee-flavoured Lemsip rather than Lemsip-flavoured coffee. The long day of rehearsals whizzed by with a caffeine-, paracetamol- and decongestant-induced energy.

This was not an especially unusual month for me – the variety of jobs, juggling more than one project at a time, is expected of conductors. I know many who take on much more. Sometimes I'm at home for a few weeks or a month, preparing music for the next rush of engagements, and personally I need and value those quieter times. During that autumn I had worked with about two hundred musicians, the majority of whom I'd never met before. In a few months

I was to travel to Calgary to make music with another hundred or so Canadian folk.

As a child I could never have imagined I would become a conductor, but there's something about pursuing this strangest of careers that somehow wouldn't have surprised my childhood self. I loved music, I loved entertaining and interacting with people, I wanted to travel, and I thought sitting in an office must be very boring and to be avoided at all costs. I have found a varied career that ticks all those boxes. Stressful and uncertain though it can be at times, it is never dull, and I cannot imagine a time when I would stop learning.

Have you seen the viral YouTube clip of three-year-old Jonathan conducting Beethoven's Fifth Symphony? It's been doing the rounds since at least 2010. He's conducting along to a recording, which isn't what we do (we lead the music rather than react to what we hear), but he's brilliant nonetheless. He has some interesting moves too – learned from watching conductors probably. The dramatic wiping of the brow is excellent, though I'm not sure where he got the nose-picking from, and that really distracts him for a few bars. It's obvious he's grown up with classical music in the house and I'm guessing he's already learning an instrument. More impressive still is his strong sense of the structure – the push and pull of the musical narrative, the moments of drama. He mutters something in excitement as the huge *crescendo* grows and tension builds then explodes into the joyous C major finale. He knows exactly when it's going to happen, and that's impressive. But what is the envy of many musicians is his sheer uninhibited joy. It's physical, the music is in his hands, and in his whole body. The symphony ends with a hilariously large number of 'final' chords – as if Beethoven just can't bear to end the piece. Jonathan finds this so funny he ends up falling off his little podium and rolling around on the floor in fits of giggles. I don't think an orchestra would thank a conductor for that, but you get the idea.

Most of us 'musos' will remember how we fell in love with music – the first time we heard a live orchestra, an operatic voice or a string quartet, and there was no going back. Or maybe we grew up surrounded by it, and it has always been as lovable and familiar as a close relative. We can't imagine living without it. We will have a story to tell as to how this art form captured us as children and how we caught the life-long bug. Then, very early in our training, we rightly understand that no matter how much we love it, to create that magic we shall have endless technical skills to hone. If we don't learn this, if we don't practise (and that never stops throughout our lives), we shall just play wrong notes, make an unpleasant sound, and the magic will very quickly disappear. It's not enough to put us off, and we still love it and even relish the hard work involved. But along the way, do we lose the joy that Jonathan so clearly shows?

I played this short video at the start of my conducting workshops in Dublin and Oxford, as I do for all those starter workshops. It always makes them laugh. Next comes a short clip of my teacher – the legendary Russian conductor and pedagogue Ilya Alexandrovich Musin. He was ninety-three at the time the video was made, and he too is conducting Beethoven. I can see the technical brilliance in every gesture, but what strikes everyone is the 'Jonathan joy'. It's on his face, in his whole body. Ninety years of hard work, analysis, life and wisdom between them, but they share that joy of the music. I ask the participants to remember that – to hold onto it every time they feel locked in and fearful.

Conducting is a multi-skilled job, requiring razor-sharp hearing, musical and intellectual discipline, imagination, excellent time-management (micro and macro), and intense periods of score preparation – hours, days, weeks, months and years of study. All the above should be a given, but most importantly conductors need excellent communication skills, otherwise their musical knowledge and ideas will stay right there in their heads. The language used to communicate in rehearsal is both verbal and visual, with more emphasis on the latter. In the performance it is entirely visual. It is partly a technical language and means of expression, yet the conductor's personality cannot help but shine through – flaws and all!

As well as practical information, orchestras are looking for inspiration from their conductor, who is in effect a salesperson for the music and their interpretation. On rare occasions, in the very finest orchestral performances, the conductor totally embodies the music – a vessel through which the music flows. And there is a fine line here. Conductors produce no sound at all – bar the odd grunt (you can hear that on recordings sometimes, but it hardly adds to the performance). Yet they aren't just dancing to the music. Their gestures should be leading the musicians in creating the sound and not just keeping the ensemble together, so a physically uninhibited conductor is helpful. Having said that, an emoting, out-of-control arm-flapper is the most annoying creature on earth to an orchestral player, however much it might impress the audience. Conducting gestures should embody conflicting elements – rhythmic accuracy versus sound, mood and expression. Classical musicians typically spend years focusing on producing sounds, and not caring so much about their appearance. This changes when we become conductors. The orchestral sound is reflected in a conductor's physicality. It is no longer about how to make contact with an instrument, but how to make contact with the air, how we move silently through space. It needs to be controlled yet uninhibited. Even our facial expressions will be read, consciously or otherwise, by an orchestra. We are leaders, and like all good leaders, we are listening keenly and responding in the moment. It's really a very difficult job.

My views, explanations, passions, aspects of the job I particularly love, these are as peculiar to me as my own conducting style. By telling my story, and interviewing some of my most trusted colleagues, I attempt to explain this elusive art, describing the variety of ways in which a modern conductor can earn a living and enjoy a successful career. This is not a handbook for conductors, but in attempting to describe what I do, there are small sections that fall into that category. Feel free to ignore them if they become too technical or indeed not technical enough.

I am British and live in London. While there is a big international side to my work, and I spent seven years living abroad, there is an inevitable emphasis in the book on the UK. However, of the sixteen conductors I interviewed, six are non-British and two have dual nationality. I deliberately chose from a relatively diverse background – nine women, three conductors from black and ethnically diverse backgrounds, and with an age range of nearly fifty years. Classical music is certainly international, though it would be disingenuous to say this wholly reflects the industry and conducting profession, which still woefully lacks inclusivity. Yet we are making slow progress, and I wanted to celebrate that. I also chose not just big names, but a variety of working conductors, at different stages in their careers. Becoming a successful conductor in fact only rarely involves wealth and fame, though I believe it is one of the richest and most fulfilling jobs imaginable.

Part I

1: The Start

Time to Play

I am a privileged middle-class white woman with all the advantages that gives me in life. My father was a clergyman and my mother a primary school teacher. Until just before my tenth birthday, I enjoyed an idyllic, carefree, playful childhood in a Norfolk rectory with acres of garden. There was plenty of music. My parents had met as students at Trinity College of Music in London. My father sang, played the guitar and lute, and had a very sophisticated knowledge of harmony and counterpoint. My mother played the piano and was a supremely gifted children's choir director. Dad was an eccentric, liberal-minded and charismatic priest. He wasn't evangelical, though he'd talk with very great enthusiasm about his faith and his many doubts. The rectory had an open door. Parishioners could drop in at any time, and my sister and I were comfortable talking to anyone of any age and background.

It was a well-educated family, yet I somehow managed to hide from my parents that I couldn't read terribly well, and although I sang in the church choir and played the trumpet, I *certainly* couldn't read music. It was the 1970s, SATS and assessments didn't exist, and my mother taught at another school, so faking it was quite possible.

We cycled around the local villages, played in our large garden and sometimes next door in the creepy graveyard, overlooked by the cavernous, architecturally rich medieval church of St Agnes, Cawston. Classroom time in the local primary school was quite dull, and we lived for playtime in our enormous school playing field. A passionate sailor, my father bought a small dinghy and took us sailing on the Norfolk Broads and the North Sea. We were adventurous with no sense that some things girls just 'can't do'. Those years were very happy and the fact that we were free to roam and feed our imaginations was, I believe, key to our development, and we caught up on the other aspects of education eventually. My sister and I were confident, articulate, happy and healthy children. The salary of a clergyman and a part-time teacher was small, but it was a rich childhood, nonetheless.

On 17 April 1980, my father drowned in a sailing accident off the north Norfolk coast and our lives were turned upside down. My sister and some family friends' children were involved and nearly died too, and I watched the whole thing unfold from the shore. I remember it vividly, and part of my childhood and self-confidence was left on the shore that day. Within months we had to move from the rectory and consequently moved schools. In the following months I used to stop what I was doing and ask myself if I would be doing it if Dad was still alive. By September, almost nothing I did, nowhere I went, was the same.

Clergy and their dependants are not wealthy but there are charities to help keep them in middle-class comfort and education. The archaically named Clergy Orphan Corporation swung into action and offered to pay fees at a nearby prep school, Beeston Hall. I was put into a very academically bright class with children a year younger than me, and I remained a year behind right the way through my school education. Looking back, I can see there were sound, well-meaning reasons for this, though no one thought to explain them to me, or even to tell me that this was going to happen. I found out when on my first day we went round the class saying how old we were and I figured out that I must be very stupid. Probably not the greatest boost in confidence to a little girl who'd just lost her dad, but I was quickly learning resilience and to keep these upsets to myself. Eventually I convinced myself that being given that extra year was just what I needed to realise my musical and intellectual potential, and I still believe that. But it took me many years to get rid of the idea that I was behind and therefore slower than my contemporaries.

St Margaret's

In 1982 I quite happily went as a boarder and a 'foundationer' to St Margaret's School in Bushey, Hertfordshire. Founded in 1749 for the 'fatherless daughters of the clergy', by the 1980s there were just eleven clergy orphans, and the rest were 'normal' fee-paying girls. It sounds like something grim from a Brontë novel, but the reality for me was mostly positive. Some would be surprised to hear this, but going away to school, being taken away from the responsibilities of home for some of the time, was good for me. I felt freer from worry and missed my dad less, yet I never felt unloved, and the holidays with my mother and sister were always the best times of the year. Also, there were other clergy orphans at the school, and we understood each other. I'm still close friends with some of them. At Beeston I felt embarrassed at my dad not being alive. It seems extraordinary, but it was just too hard to deal with the reaction of my peers when I said that my dad was dead – it made me feel 'other'. At St Margaret's I could just say I was a 'foundationer' and everyone knew what that meant, and it didn't bother them.

As in other schools, there was a handful of horrendously cruel members of staff, and, looking back, some bizarrely mean-spirited school rules, but there were many kind and clever people educating and caring for us too. There were eccentric, enlightened, super-bright older women who had dedicated their life to teaching and had some wonderful nuggets of wisdom to impart. The education was overall pretty good, and I did a lot of sport too, which saved me from being too 'square'. 'Alice has indefatigable stick work' was my lacrosse report – perhaps that could be my strapline today. Bushey is near London, so school trips to concerts, theatres and museums were frequent. It was all very wholesome.

There were pupils from Nigeria, Hong Kong, India and even Libya and Iran, as well as a lot of Jewish girls who lived locally and so didn't board. Sadly, we weren't encouraged to learn about their cultures and religions, and I regret that lost opportunity. They were to go to chapel and become 'nice English girls'. It was a church school, but not evangelical; attending chapel was an endurance but they weren't expected to convert to Christianity, and I suppose this was something their parents had chosen for them. It could have been worse, but I feel embarrassed by the endemic unconscious racism.

It was of course music that made me most happy and fulfilled, and I could ignore the less attractive sides of boarding-school life by throwing myself into this. Since Dad's death, music had taken on a great importance. In those few remaining months at Cawston rectory, I sat down with a recorder and *Singing Together* (that accompanying booklet to the iconic BBC Radio Music Education programme) and played through every tune until I became fluent. I started the piano a year after my father died. That's quite late for someone who ends up becoming a professional musician, but it was the right time for me, and I practised obsessively, rattling through the grades in just a few years. Life was serious and deeper now and like many children who experience loss, music was an outlet for emotions I couldn't put into words.

At St Margaret's I practically lived in the music department and was able to practise the organ, trumpet and piano at every spare moment – day and night. The award-winning chapel choir rehearsed almost daily. We were the rent-a-choir for many boys' schools and joined forces for big choral works. By the time I left the school, I had sung nearly all the giants of the repertoire from Handel's *Messiah* to Britten's *War Requiem*.

We had an inspiring music director called Graham Garton. Very much the captain of the ship, he encouraged us to punch above our weight. He wrote a new grace every week, which we sang before Wednesday lunch, and with chapel services, competitions and concerts, we were all good sight-readers. It was as close as you could get to a cathedral choir school, an option still open only to boys. Yet it was nowhere near as immersive, and the fact that we as girls all had to accept this privilege was bestowed only on boys was rarely questioned.

My parents partly jokingly said they had always planned to have two boys and send them to choir school. Both my sister and I could make as nice a noise as the boys, and we were very keen, but in the 1970s there was no questioning the wisdom of the Church of England in ignoring this talent and enthusiasm. My dad ran the church choir, and it was full of very good girls and young women, and a smattering of somewhat reluctant boys. My parents once took us to evensong at King's College, Cambridge, and I think it was the first time I experienced real envy. Watching those little boys all dressed up, so assured (and, let's face it, looking a bit pompous), I wanted that life very badly. There's plenty of examples of excellent singers and conductors in the operatic and symphonic world coming from this background. For some, the aesthetic and technical challenge of moving from cerebral church music to these more visceral forms of expression is not for them. However, there's no doubting the solid musical grounding a cathedral choir training and education can give.

When I was fifteen, I started to attend the Oundle International Organ Week, and quickly realised I was behind the many ex-cathedral choristers around me. They seemed to have knowledge of repertoire, musicianship and general self-belief in abundance, though I could see even then that I was perhaps more at ease talking on a variety of subjects beyond Bach, Messiaen and organ-pipe wind pressures. I was told by tutors on these courses that I was good enough to apply for an Oxbridge organ scholarship, though – absurdly, I see now – I thought they were just being kind. One of the country's leading organists and teachers, Nicholas Danby, had agreed to teach me, and once a month I would travel to the Royal College of Music for lessons with him, courtesy of the Clergy Orphan Corporation. It was all looking very positive.

Oxford

If someone had told me when I was nineteen that I would become a professional conductor, I would never have believed them – I was just as likely to become a fighter pilot. 'An Englishman's strongest emotion is embarrassment,' my English teacher used to say. Well, how about a teenage girl in the 1980s? If the Margaret Thatcher model didn't chime (and it most certainly didn't for me), then who were our role models? Our ideas of authority, leadership and career prospects were scrambled. In theory women could do anything with their lives, but one only has to watch a clip of 1980s

TV with its outrageous casual sexism to see what confusing mixed messages we were receiving. My teenage self is positively in awe of the wisdom and sophistication of many of today's teenagers, though I am sure the embarrassment strain is still there. Embarrassment, or rather self-consciousness and inhibition, was debilitating for me as a teenage musician, and an element of that has haunted me for many decades. Not until my forties was I able to let go and really let the music out. I had finally come home. Yes, it really was a homecoming. A core element of my personality that I had left behind three decades ago was re-emerging. Confidence both personal and professional, internal and external, life and perhaps a little bit of wisdom all contributed to the real me daring to show itself.

In 1989 I went to Oxford University holding an organ scholarship at St Hugh's College. There are many British conductors who start out that way, so on paper it wouldn't have been such a leap. Depending on the size and prestige of the college chapel choir, Oxbridge organ scholars are expected either to run the music entirely themselves or to be something very close to an assistant cathedral organist, playing for all the services for a professional music director. Either way, they are supposed to act like a professional musician despite still being a teenager. Learning on the job, sinking or swimming, it is a peculiarly British approach to musical training, and one that has changed for the better in recent years. Now many colleges employ professional music directors to guide the music-making, though there's still a thriving student-led music life, and professional demands on organ scholars are still high. At St Hugh's I was very much left to my own devices in running the chapel music, which included the choir, making it up as I went along, drawing on what I'd learned from years of singing in choirs. Far from relishing this, I had so little confidence on so many levels that initially I was scared out of my wits. I'm not being falsely modest when I say that the results in that first year were not good. There were two big stumbling blocks. Waving my hands around in front of people was really embarrassing, and I assumed a conductor was supposed to know more than all the people in front of them. It being Oxford University, everyone in the choir seemed very clever from where I was standing, so this difficulty appeared insurmountable.

I'm not quite sure where I got the idea that a conductor (even a student conductor) must know everything, but it was entrenched. The university was full of aspiring conductors, conducting their college choirs and orchestras, starting their own, or winning auditions to conduct the main university orchestras. It never occurred to me that these would-be conductors (many of whom were becoming close friends), who talked about this art form with such authority and enthusiasm, didn't know much more than me. Nor did they claim to know more than anyone else; they were just daring to step onto the podium and have a go. It was me who replaced the podium with a pedestal and decided their brilliance was unattainable to me.

I got into Oxford to study for a degree in Classics. The organ scholarship was extra-curricular, and was clearly where my interests lay, but that I could become a professional musician seemed fanciful. 'Keep it as a hobby' was very sensible British advice I'd heard a lot. I remember the school careers adviser, exasperated and amused in equal measure at my psychometric career test results. I had resolutely refused to tick any box that implied financial gain was more important than job satisfaction. 'Good Lord, I can see you an impoverished musician, walking the streets with an instrument in your hand!' I didn't think I was a good enough to be a musician, I loved A-level Latin and Greek and totally convinced myself and even managed to convince the Classics tutors at St Hugh's that this was a good idea. But the leap from A level to 'Mods & Greats', the famous Oxford Classics degree that was said to be harder than Japanese business exams, was terrifying and frankly beyond me. 'You can get any job with that degree,' we were all told. 'Computer programming, law, finance, politics, teaching, spying . . . It shows you can do anything.' I can do only things that engage me, so that ruled out most of the list, though maybe spying . . . but judging from the books and TV dramas, those characters all seemed a bit lonely and miserable.

I was by no means a straight-A student. I did well in most subjects, but I had to work very hard, and I really needed that extra year. I think I inherited some of my father's severe dyslexia. I must have it a bit because just now it took me four attempts to write 'dyslexia' before the auto-correct could even recognise the word. I stumble when reading aloud, find reading to myself effortful, don't know my right from my left and often jumble up numbers. I don't *make* careless mistakes. I just don't *see* the mistakes.

I quickly recognised my heart wasn't in Classics and was disinclined to attempt coasting along. So, after a year of translating and writing about Homer and Virgil, Greek plays, ancient history, philosophy and looking at pots and statues, I changed to Music and started my degree all over again. The imposter syndrome continued but it was my issue, since my wonderful tutor, Dr John Warrack, couldn't have been more welcoming. It was 1990 and I was twenty – now *two* years behind most of my year.

During my two first years, it gradually dawned on me that perhaps a conductor didn't need to know absolutely everything to galvanise a group at least to start and finish at the same time. The real turning point was when it fell to me to conduct Fauré's Requiem with St Hugh's College Music Society. The handful of music undergraduates in the college was expected to take charge of the extra-curricular music. We could be as adventurous as we wanted, with a small budget, most of which went on the after-concert party – a bribe to draw in musicians. A little bit of competitiveness kicked in, and I didn't want to be left out as we shared the opportunities.

I felt an impending gloom at the thought of every rehearsal, yet as soon as I was rehearsing, I was in the moment with these musicians. My nerves disappeared, and my only focus was to make music and to get that music sounding better than it did at the start. I always left the rehearsal on a high. I had learned a magically simple trick to help a musical ensemble start together – taking a breath (see Chapter 2). With this up my sleeve, and having made sure I learned the score well, I was ready for the concert. The entrepreneurial music scene at Oxford had allowed me to observe much. Anyone who wanted to conduct their favourite work could normally expect to get a group together to do so. As a trumpeter, I'd played in many of these concerts, and experienced some excellent and also some truly terrible music-making. Whatever the results, the person at the head seemed refreshingly unapologetic. By this time, I'd gained some of that famous Oxbridge arrogance and this helped bat away some of my self-doubt.

Something wonderful happened in the concert itself. My nerves disappeared, and I simply enjoyed the music. So often my nerves had been debilitating, no matter how well prepared I was, and performances were never as good as they were behind closed doors. I was beginning to think that I just didn't have the performing gene, though for some reason I continued to put myself through hell and seek out opportunities to play in public. And why had I chosen two exceptionally noisy instruments, if I was so shy? There was always another kind of noise that accompanied me through an organ recital or a service, reminding me that I might screw it up at any moment. If I played a trumpet solo in an orchestra, a little demon was there to remind me that I could easily split that exposed note just coming up, turning it from the dramatic climax of the work to a comedy musical raspberry. In fact, this rarely happened, but it led to my playing it safe and giving a reserved, controlled and ultimately boring performance.

Some people think that conducting has got to be the most nerve-racking of all musical disciplines. Yet conducting has some key elements that help combat nerves. Firstly, you have your back to the audience. Secondly, the nerve-wracking bit is meeting a new orchestra for the first time and gaining the trust of the musicians. The rehearsals are the test. The performance, though not without some stress, is the fun bit – the icing on the cake. And, of course, a conductor can't play wrong notes.

Everyone was surprised at the success of the Fauré Requiem performance. Instead of the clamour of self-doubts going on inside my head, my focus was external – the music and the performers. We had rehearsed, and I knew what to do. I wasn't worried for myself, nor was I worried for anyone else. A Haydn 'Nelson' Mass and Mozart C minor Mass followed in my final year, and I had well and truly caught the conducting bug.

2: The Basics:
Hands and Baton

Waving

Whenever someone introduces me in a social situation and says I'm a conductor, they invariably do some waving gestures, mirroring their hands, performing a little conductor mime. It happens all the time. Is it to differentiate us from the bus conductor? Yes, we get the 'So you work on the buses' joke a lot. In fact, the waving of hands is fundamental to the art.

As a teenager my fear, before I ever attempted to conduct, was simply: How on earth can I get a group of people to start making music at the same time? This is the most basic and essential job of a conductor. It was worse than that. I didn't believe they would start at all, let alone together. I fully expected them to stare back at me, utterly bewildered at my panicked, meaningless flailing. To this day, although that fear has long disappeared, it remains a recurring anxiety dream. I once dreamed I resorted to stabbing a double-bass player to stop them playing, so it would seem that worried me too. The performance starting without me while I'm trying to find the concert hall regularly crops up in dreams too. The result when I was finally forced to take the plunge with my college chapel choir wasn't quite that bad. It was a small choir, they were kind people, and decent musicians, so they helped me out.

Remembering to breathe, a clear and decisive breath, is the conductor's best friend and was a revelation to me. How often do we forget that most essential act? Of course, we breathe all the time, but often it is shallow, especially when we're nervous. When we sing or play a wind or brass instrument, we breathe to make the noise, but in fact all musicians need breath. Even organists, who have huge artificial wind forces at the touch of a button, should breathe as they are about to start a phrase. If that breath is related to the tempo and character of the phrase about to be played, then the body will more likely follow suit.

A Mini-Guide for the Curious

How to Start

Try this:

Sing the first line of the chorus 'We All Live in a Yellow Submarine' and, as you do so, make your preparatory breath audible. Now grab a friend. Ask them to sing it with you but tell them that you are to decide when you are both start. Smile, look them in the eye (in a friendly, non-threatening way) and make that audible breath again. Did you start together? Grab more friends and repeat.

Do the breathing trick again, and this time as you make that breath, raise your dominant hand (left or right, it doesn't matter, whatever the purists say) and drop it lightly down on the 'W' of 'We'.

Repeat, but this time use both hands.

The conductor's baton-holding hand (their dominant hand) does a lot more work than the other as it usually beats time all the way through. The other hand comes in and out when needed, helping with phrasing and character, and cue-ing instruments. Mirroring the dominant hand with the non-dominant one all the way through isn't cool, despite it being the mime everyone uses to describe a conductor. But if you start with just one hand it can look as though only half your body is engaged in the activity. Two hands at the start looks more confident and committed.

Try to keep the breath as natural as possible, think about the song you are about to sing, the speed you would like to sing it, the character of the song, rather than the breath itself. What you want to avoid is that type of breath we take – holding tensely and releasing in a burst – as we jump into cold water. That will cause the musical equivalent of a messy splash.

Once we have the musicians starting together, then we need to keep them together and not allow them to go off at different speeds. However, there is a lot of information written on the orchestral players' pages that means they don't need to keep staring at the conductor all the way through, for every second of the piece.

Beating Time

Anyone who has learned an instrument at school in the UK might well have done at least one or two grade exams. Back in the day you had to 'conduct along' to a piece of music, showing whether it had two, three or four beats or pulses in a bar. The pulse would either have a dance-like feeling of three inside each pulse (think 'Ring-a-Ring o' Roses') or a march-like feeling of two (think 'The Grand Old Duke of York'). And you would indicate where the strong beats come, i.e. on the first beat of the bar – the downbeat. Two-in-a-bar was up and down; three was a triangle, and four was a type of up-side-down 'T' with an extra triangle to take you back to the downbeat. It was all very stiff and earnest and had little to do with the flow of music, but musicians grow up knowing these important basic shapes.

There is an element of this in conducting, but most importantly our job is to lead the music rather than beat along in time. Time-beating is merely reacting to what you hear. Conductors should be particularly clear with the downbeat, and that downbeat can be crucial for signalling to the orchestra where we are in the musical phrase.

Well over a hundred years ago, composers started using more complicated time signatures. By the early twentieth century, bars in five and seven are commonplace. The beats sound quirky and uneven because they can't be divided equally. For example, they start mixing the pulse of 'Ring-a-Ring o' Roses' with 'The Grand Old Duke of York' in one bar. Harder to dance to, but characterful. Nowadays we have all sorts of complicated time signatures (e.g. three and a half beats in a bar), and these can keep changing. Sometimes every bar in a phrase will have a different time signature. If the pulse of the music is slow, we sometimes need to subdivide the beat. For example, a very slow four in a bar might need to be beaten in eight because your hands just can't move from beat to beat that slowly, and it's harder to keep the ensemble together. Deciding whether to subdivide is usually up to the conductor and is to do with the shaping of the phrase. Too much subdivision can look overly busy, involve unnecessary micro-managing, and usually results in an unintended slowing down.

Those of you who sat those tortuous music theory exams (which most children who become conductors actually love) will know that the international music language is Italian, and words such as *Allegro* and *Adagio* tell us approximately at what speed to play. Sometimes changes in tempo happen suddenly, at other times gradually. A few centuries ago composers began to add metronome markings, which more precisely indicate the speed they want – 60, 92 or 112 beats per minute, etc. That seems exact, but they are still just indications, and rarely a precise demand. Musicians can interpret this for themselves but for a group to sound together, it falls to the conductor to decide.

Within a symphony there can be moments where the music stops on a held note (a *fermata*) and will restart. Once they start or have restarted, orchestral players won't be looking at every single beat. They can count just as well as the conductor, but they need to know the beat is reliable and clear, particularly if the music is rhythmically complex, and they might be too far away from some instruments to hear them. Individual players will be looking up at different times, and many if not most of the conductor's gestures will be absorbed by their peripheral vision. Orchestral players have a peripheral vision (watching the conductor, their music, other musicians) equal to that of a professional footballer. The players' and conductor's peripheral hearing are working intensely as well. We can't just be on the same page, or the same bar, or the same beat; we need to be exactly to a nanosecond on the same beat. That person at the front should ensure that everything holds together.

Expression

Clear hand gestures are required just to make sure the ensemble is good, and it doesn't sound a mess. Yet that is only part of it. What we also need to show is the volume, quality and strength of sound, the character, the mood, the atmosphere, and these aspects change throughout most pieces. Composers often write Italian words to help us with this (*piano, pianissimo, forte, fortissimo, espressivo, dolce,* etc.) but they are relative and open to interpretation. How to convey that to an orchestra? A certain amount of acting is involved.

Volume

Try this:

Conduct the first line of 'We All Live in a Yellow Submarine' with your breath and hands as before, and put a volume to it – loud, soft, very soft, very very soft, medium loud, etc. Did you find your gestures were bigger when loud?

Sound

As a child of the 1970s I well remember the BBC Schools broadcast *Music and Movement*. At seven years of age, my embarrassment levels were low, but even I felt a bit silly leaping around the school hall with my classmates in a leotard pretending to be a big loud growly tiger, or a tiny quiet mouse. Or even more baffling: a tree!!?? Working in theatre and particularly opera training, I have watched many warm-ups and workshops run by stage directors and choreographers. When appropriate, I join in. All very *Music and Movement* and one must leave embarrassment at the door. Many conductors, particularly of the older generation, while respecting that the singers need to do this, are utterly allergic to the idea of participation, seeing it as undignified and frankly silly. I'm told by some who worked for the English Opera Group that Benjamin Britten always took part in physical warm-ups at the start of rehearsals he was conducting. If it's good enough for one of the greatest composers of the twentieth century, then it's good enough for me. There are situations where it's best to leave the singers and stage director to get on with this alone, and a conductor's presence can be off-putting. But, in the right setting, it's a wonderful way of allowing the company to gel and presents a place of mutual trust. I've also learned a great deal from this and unapologetically use it in my teaching.

Children's education in music and movement is way more imaginative and fun now, but even today, as early as toddlerhood, we associate big with loud and small with quiet.

That can be useful with conducting, but there's a more subtle element if we also think about the quality of sound in terms of weight and texture. Singing or playing quietly can require more effort and control, so shrinking your gestures can make musicians feel tense and restricted, particularly in their breathing. This is the last thing they need. Better to think of 'quiet' as light, and 'loud' as heavy, dense.

Try this:

As you take your breath and raise your hand, imagine grabbing something on the upbeat and placing or throwing it down on the 'W' of 'We'. If you want 'We all live' to be loud, then imagine picking up something heavy like a rock, and if quiet, something light like a feather. Imagine picking up different objects in between of varying weights and material. The type of object should affect the way your hands move and consequently the way the sound comes out. A needle and a feather are just as light but should make a completely different type of 'W' – the former would be soft, the latter pointed. A heavy rock would probably make a harsh sound whereas a thick cloth a warm thick sound.

Conducting Charades
Try this:

Conduct the first line of 'We all live' either with a friend or in front of the mirror. This time put an adjective to it: happy, sad, joyful, miserable, sombre, grandiose – choose your own. Take a breath and move your hands in this character. Show the adjective in your facial expression. You might find some adjectives require bigger hand and arm gestures. If you're struggling with this, or find it a bit embarrassing, try these two: relaxed, over-confident.

See if your friend can guess the adjective from your gestures. Ask them if it affects the way they sing. Did it also affect the speed and volume you sang it at? Probably.

Try to combine the charades and the object. Pick up a rock in an aggressive way, a feather in a carefree way, a rock in a carefree way, a feather in an aggressive way.

Ending a phrase or a piece requires similar thought. Will the cut-off be gentle or strong? What kind of character?

What we strive for in our hands and our whole body is to convey a perfect, ever-changing balance of clear rhythm and expression. Orchestras are rarely enthusiastic about conductors who just beat time. Yet a conductor who gives them all the musical imagery but makes their life hard when they need rhythmic clarity can be equally frustrating.

The Baton

In just about every film that I've watched involving a scene with an orchestra rehearsing, the conductor will tap the music stand and the hitherto noisy group will immediately fall silent and become an attentive orchestra ready to play. It's strange because I certainly don't do that, and I can't think of anyone who would. It's a bit impolite; a baton is built to move through air and hitting something hard might break it; and most importantly tapping it won't be heard. Normally the orchestra will fall silent when the leader stands up and indicates for the oboist to play the 'A' for everyone to tune to. If there is still noise once they have tuned, then a confident 'Good morning/afternoon' or, if you've already greeted them, just 'OK' is all one needs. But the image of this all-powerful stick, this wand, is what everyone associates with a conductor. There's something about holding the stick in your hand that makes you feel like a conductor, and it can be a useful psychological prop when you're starting out, but it can do more damage than good if you don't know how to use it.

Normally when I teach a beginner conductor, or someone who has been conducting for a while but hasn't taken lessons, I will recommend they start without the baton. To get their hands really into the music, to have that sensation of holding the sound and moving it around, it is easier not to be worrying about the stick. The baton should be an extension of your hands and fingers. It's especially useful with music that needs rhythmic precision or with large ensembles, and it can add to the repertoire of gestures. A small movement in your hands and fingers will be magnified by the baton, and that's great when your hands are working, but can create havoc when things are not quite in place.

Conducting in the seventeenth century was a far less subtle art of bashing a long stick on the floor to keep time. The French composer Jean-Baptiste Lully accidentally bashed his foot so hard in a performance that he developed a gangrenous infection that eventually killed him. Fortunately, this dangerous and unsubtle tradition of conducting died out and the delicate baton we recognise today evolved more from the violin bow. As still happens today in some ensembles, the orchestral leader (often called the concert master) would direct the players from the front desk of the violins, sometimes standing. This, along with leading from the keyboard, is how the conductor emerged over the centuries. There's something about the grip of the baton and connection with the sound that can feel very like playing a string instrument.

There are conductors who don't use a baton, preferring that 'hands-on' feeling. They can be just as precise without the baton but personally I find it very useful and use it pretty much all the time. My teacher in Russia would encourage us all to switch between the two – some weeks or months with, some without. The important thing is to avoid tensing up when holding it as this can lead to injuries such as tennis elbow. When it becomes as natural as an extension of your fingers rather than an inanimate object, one can understand why it looks a bit like a wizard weaving magic.

In fact, the best baton shop in the UK is not unlike Ollivanders, the wand shop in the Harry Potter books. Just off Regent's Street in London, J. P. Guivier and Co. is most famous for its string instruments, but it also has a wonderful collection of batons. These come in different lengths and shapes of handle, and most conductors find their 'one' and continue to buy that model for the rest of their career. Or does the baton find them? They are wooden and for decades they were made by two carpenters – a father and son. They cost £13.50, and a smart wooden case with a velvet interior costs £35. A case is essential because they break easily, but a cardboard or plastic poster tube would do just as well. Starting out on a conducting career can be expensive but buying this bit of equipment is not, at least if compared with the cost of an instrument.

An injury from this little stick is unlikely to require amputation these days, but they are quite sharp. I once had some explaining to do when going through security at the airport. Although batons are not made of metal, they could still do some damage. Some conductors prefer the fibreglass baton, which is tougher and heavier. Self-inflicted injuries do occur (accidental hand-stabbing or one horrendous story of a baton going up a nose) but these are fortunately rare incidents. I have never injured myself but early in my career, to avoid tensing, in a few performances my grip was so relaxed that the baton flew out of my hand and into the audience. Luckily it never landed on an expensive instrument.

I've broken the tops of a few when conducting an opera in a covered pit. In extra enthusiastic upbeats it made contact with the ceiling. When I studied in Russia, I was a cat-sitter for an eccentric long-haired Russian Blue who was convinced my endless baton waving was a game purely for his enjoyment. If I left my batons lying around the flat, they'd get chewed up.

3: Lighting the Fire

Life-changing Concerts

It was 1982, and I was sitting in Watford Town Hall with a small group of friends from school, listening and watching our English teacher's brother Philip Fowke play Tchaikovsky's Piano Concerto No. 1 with the London Philharmonic Orchestra. Despite my musical upbringing, there were gaps, and this was the first time I had heard a world-class symphony orchestra play live with a world-class soloist in a world-class acoustic. I don't remember the rest of the programme as it was the concerto that spoke to me that night, that thrilled me to the bone. I just couldn't believe classical music could be so gratifying, exciting, and downright flamboyant. What an opening! I had grown to adore pieces of music through repetition, either listening or playing, but this was instantaneous. I wanted more of this luxurious Romantic sound world, and I knew it was far removed from anything I could make myself. I could hear the big difference between the LPO and any orchestra I was lucky enough to play in. I wanted to be part of this world but had no idea how and knew at best it was not going to happen any time soon. Could I be the piano soloist? Unlikely, and in any case it was the orchestral sound I was most in love with. How about the organ? Well, yes, in just a few years I would have opportunities to make rich orchestral sounds on large instruments in huge resonant buildings. I even taught myself to play the organ and trumpet at the same time – holding the trumpet in my right hand, leaving my left hand and feet for the organ, and pulling out stops with the bell of the trumpet. Yet the organ isn't quite the living, breathing organism that is the orchestra. The conducting option just never occurred to me. I don't think that was down to gender, as I was proudly ignoring the stereotypes with the trumpet and organ, and I'd seen Jane Glover conducting plenty of times on the TV. That twelve-year-old girl would never have expected to find herself in Sweden twenty years later conducting that very Tchaikovsky concerto.

I realised this would need to be a listening adventure, and a solitary one at that. Even in an old-fashioned girls' boarding school in the 1980s, it wasn't cool to love this kind of music. The advent of the Sony Walkman was useful, but I had to remember not to turn the volume up too high with my cheap leaky headphones. When my friends were listening to Wham! and Culture Club, I guiltily and secretly listened to Elgar and Mendelssohn. In the holidays I commandeered the record-player at home and obsessively watched the Proms on TV over the summer. Attending LPO concerts at Watford Town Hall became a regular pastime, and another exciting music world was opening up.

———

For Barry Wordsworth it was also the LPO, at his local swimming baths, drained, covered and transformed into a temporary concert hall:

> It was Sir Adrian Boult conducting the *Enigma Variations*. I had a fantastic music master called Charles Cleall, and at the end of the lesson the next day he said, 'Wordsworth, what have you been dreaming about all morning? I can't get any sense out of you.' I told him all about this fantastic concert. He knew Sir Adrian, and he said, 'I'll write to him and tell him what you just said.' I was appalled and embarrassed. But he did, and two weeks later a letter arrived from his life-long secretary Gwendoline Beckett saying, 'Sir Adrian Boult bids me tell you that he would like to meet you.' And that's how our friendship started. He became a great mentor to me.

Marin Alsop was nine when she first saw the man who was to become her mentor and hero on the podium:

> I found classical music very off-putting. Not my parents, they were hip, if you can call parents 'hip'. There were too many rules, and not enough fun. I loved playing in the orchestra, but got into trouble for moving, talking, and smiling too much. Then my dad took me to a concert and that was the first time I saw [Leonard] Bernstein conducting. He was jumping around and talking to us

– the audience. That was the fun and engaging classical music I wanted to do.

Children growing up in large cities – like Ben Glassberg – are far more likely to be exposed to large-scale symphonic concerts:

Living in London, it was so easy to hear amazing concerts, and I went to a lot, but it was seeing Philippe Jordan conducting in a concert of Mozart and Mahler when I was twelve that made think, 'I want to be a conductor.'

Starts and False Starts

I was about nine years old and had been learning the cornet for about six months when I was dropped off at an Oddfellows Hall in a neighbouring north Norfolk town to join a rehearsal of their silver band. I don't remember much about it, except that it mostly comprised old men, a few scary women, and surly teenagers. I was given a seat and music was placed on the stand in front of me. I had no idea what to do, I don't believe anyone spoke to me after that, and I am not sure I made a single sound the whole evening. I lasted just one rehearsal. Happily, this unhelpful experience was merely a false start and didn't put me off for long. A few years later I was to become a founding member of the National Children's Wind Orchestra of Great Britain, and the joy of playing in orchestras was something I quickly came to love even more than singing in choirs.

My father had found a silver cornet (made by Boosey and old enough to predate the merger with Hawkes) in an antique shop in Norwich. I had shown an interest in learning a brass instrument, although I can see now that my parents were kindly, thoughtfully and deliberately pushing me in that direction. My sister, clearly having a natural affinity for the cello, found she could immediately strum away on a guitar, and get a tune on any stringed instrument she picked up. The last thing they wanted was for me to feel compared unfavourably with her, and the cornet suited my somewhat outgoing personality. They made encouraging noises at the windy noises I produced, which to be fair weren't too bad for a beginner. I could at least get a note almost straight away, and tunes followed. Later, with the long-term hope that I'd be able to play in an orchestra, they bought me a cheap but functioning trumpet. My parents would not let my sister touch my instruments, so I was free to muddle along at my own pace. I really do appreciate their motives and excellent parenting, but I do wish I'd learned a stringed instrument – all that amazing repertoire!

Although the trumpet quickly became my second or even third instrument to the piano and organ, and I never practised enough to have much stamina, my teacher Ray Todd (a stalwart member of the Salvation Army) gave me a decent technique. My first ever paid job in music, at fourteen, was playing offstage trumpet in Verdi's Requiem with the Watford

Philharmonic Society at Watford Town Hall. I was paid the grand sum of £5. Right through until my early twenties, I found my way into some decent youth, student and amateur orchestras. I was rarely first trumpet, but most trumpet parts come with some responsibility, and there's no hiding in a section the way you might at the back of the strings. It's interesting how many former brass players become conductors – something to do with the daredevil attitude that's required perhaps. In contrast to the church musicians, I found the laddish behaviour of some of the brass section refreshingly straightforward and fun to be around. Of course, I simply loved the repertoire, and no matter how much noise (subtle or otherwise) I could make single-handedly on the organ, to me it felt like a pale imitation of the sound world I was experiencing as I sat in a real symphony orchestra.

Ensemble playing and singing usually starts young, with school, town, city, county and national children's and youth orchestras. As young as preschool, through to university, there have been rich opportunities for all, for the talented child determined to pursue a life in music or the curious young musician who enjoys making music but is looking for more excitement, and social and musical interaction, than can be found in practising alone. The tragedy is that these days it's only children from privileged backgrounds who can easily access this magical world and these opportunities are more frequently left to chance for less advantaged children. When free music lessons were available to every child back in the last century, so many more children fell under its spell.

Yet, despite the financial restraints, there are many pockets of music education as rich as ever, giving opportunities not just to the wealthy, both within and outside schools. Music teaching seems far more imaginative and innovative today. I doubt very much a nine-year-old child now would be made to feel as confused and unwelcome I was in that 1970s silver band.

Where Conductors are Made

Like almost all musicians, conductors belong to that lucky group of people where music appears early in their life and changes it forever. For some it's simply in the family – they are born into a world where making music is as essential as learning to walk and talk. For others, they are exposed to this world, often by an inspirational teacher in their formative years, and the fuse is lit. When interviewing my friends and colleagues I just loved hearing how it all started and saw some common themes.

ANTONIO PAPPANO: I grew up in a council flat in Pimlico. My parents were Italian immigrants working all hours and different jobs to make ends meet. My father also taught singing, there was a piano at home, and by the age of ten I was accompanying his students. We moved to Connecticut into a new chapter, society and culture. There, I met the person most influential in my early life – my piano teacher, Norma Verrilli. Alongside playing for my dad's students, I studied Bach, Mozart, Chopin, Hindemith. She also played clavichord, so I heard the music of [Heinrich] Isaac and Monteverdi. We played show tunes too. Suddenly my eyes were open to new horizons.

BARRY WORDSWORTH: My early school years I spent looking out of the window and dreaming all the time and thinking, 'What's this all about?' When I was six my parents were summoned to the headmaster. 'What are we going to do with your son?' he said, with me sitting there. Eventually, without much having been achieved, he said, 'By the way, does he sing? We need some more choirboys in the church choir.' We weren't particularly religious, but I went to the local school that had a connection to the church. The moment I stood in that choir I can remember thinking, 'Oh at last! This is what life's all about.' It was magical.

Then I got a place in the Junior Department at Trinity College of Music and had the most wonderful good luck to be taught by Gladys Puttick. We had musicianship classes every week where we did so much improvising, which was such good fun. Eight of us would line up at the two pianos, play a little bit, she'd clap her hands, the next one would sit down, and we would try to keep this improvisation going for as long as possible. She was ahead of her time. It was a wonderful education.

BRAMWELL TOVEY: I grew up in Redbridge and my family was very involved in the Salvation Army community.

So playing brass instruments was encouraged, and they realised I could from a young age replicate anything I heard on the piano. This ability was nurtured by my parents and the Salvation Army, of course.

JANE GLOVER: My brother had been a chorister at St John's, Cambridge, and I was so envious of that. I loved church music, and still do, but of course it wasn't available to girls in those days. My school had lamentable music then (now it's very good), but I did well despite it and playing the oboe in youth orchestras was wonderful.

SIAN EDWARDS: I think I only got into Oxford High School because in my interview I said, 'I like climbing trees and I want to learn the French horn.' I couldn't believe what a variety of instruments was on offer for us to learn. At the time, the headmistress, Mary Warnock [one of the country's leading philosophers], was on a mission to encourage a more diverse intake at both school and university. She wanted more musicians and sports people, and not just brilliant academics. She owned a horn and didn't have time to play, so sold it to me. There was no stopping me once I got into my first youth orchestra. Later I had some friends who put on their own concerts. In those days schools were rarely closed, and empty classrooms were available at weekends and evenings to rehearse in. My friends were heavily into Pink Floyd and the Electric Light Orchestra, and they made me a fuzzbox for my horn, so I played rock horn in some numbers, which I thought was extremely cool.

EÍMEAR NOONE: We were a typical Irish family from a tiny village of five hundred people in East Galway. My primary school teacher handed us tin whistles (in the town you got a recorder, in the countryside a penny whistle). I could play by ear and immediately started playing tunes I'd heard on TV. I was like an alien to my parents, but my teacher was adamant that I started piano lessons. It was an amazing community to grow up in and they talent spot all the time. It's not like in the US where they say, 'Honey, you can be anything you want.' In Ireland it's: 'You can do anything, but we'll let you know if it's not working.' There were always so many events, so many opportunities to perform, and there weren't enough people in the village to tell me that what I wanted to do was crazy.

LAURENCE CUMMINGS: My local church in Birmingham had two excellent choirs and there was a very good music teacher at primary school. I played flute in a school orchestra – kind of extraordinary to think the primary school had its own orchestra. And even as young as eight, I was involved in bigger projects in the city like Britten's *Noye's Fludde*. Church and school were quite a powerful combination. The 11-plus exam was big in Birmingham, and I was lucky to get into a good school with an extraordinarily high standard of music. Then my father died when I was twelve, which was very traumatic, and with the sense of responsibility I had at home I was naturally drawn to older children at school. There was a strong musical community, and they embraced me. Music was something I could completely throw myself into.

RICHARD BAKER: I was a parish church chorister in the West Midlands, and when a friend of the church organist heard me singing, she suggested I apply to Lichfield Cathedral. I was offered a scholarship, and off I went to board. I was plunged into this strange world and there were two layers that were jarring. There was the whole language of prep school, which was completely alien, and I couldn't even ask my dad about it. The problem is, the system is designed for and by the upper-middle classes. Many of the other boys were already good instrumentalists and all I could do was sing. I was quite miserable, but the way I coped with the loneliness was to write music.

After that, I went to a grammar school in Newcastle-under-Lyme. Rugby was everything there, and that wasn't my thing, yet I thrived because I was left alone to do whatever I wanted with music, and I played oboe and percussion in the county youth orchestra.

MARIA SELETSKAJA: I was born in Estonia during the Cold War, and one of the incredible things about the Soviet system was that every child had the opportunity to study at a very high level in music, sport and dance. With this horrible piano standing in every home, erratic scales were the soundtrack to the Soviet Union.

HELEN HARRISON: I grew up in Blackburn, an old cotton town, and went to an ordinary comprehensive school. My parents were teachers, but not musical. They arranged piano lessons for me, and my school gave me free violin lessons. I had a wonderful and ambitious piano teacher, and there was much music going on in the school, but it was in the Lancashire Students Symphony Orchestra I really developed. I was awarded a scholarship, had incredible training from professional musicians, and we toured abroad as well as performing locally.

TIANYI LU: I was born in China and moved to New Zealand when I was five. My parents trained as engineers (my mother later worked in insurance), but they loved music. Like many immigrants, they gave me the opportunity to learn piano to help me become well rounded, though it was very expensive for them. Later, I wanted to join the orchestra, and chose the flute (because it could fit in my bag), but also took double-bass and violin lessons as it was subsidised at secondary school. My parents were worried about my choice of career and it was a struggle to convince them to allow me to walk a path they saw as financially uncertain.

KALENA BOVELL: I grew up in the US, but my parents

are from Panama. The importance of education was drilled into us. In middle school, they put me into a beginner string class. I wanted to continue singing in the choir but it didn't fit with the schedule. The teacher asked us what we wanted to play, and because I'd had no exposure to stringed instruments I said, 'the flute'. I was handed a violin, and the first time I pulled sound I thought, 'This is me.' All I wanted to do was play the violin, and sometimes at night my parents would tell me to stop so they could get some sleep. My parents had no background in music education, and they didn't know that the next step was to take private lessons. I had my first one-to-one violin lesson when I was eighteen. I was so far behind, but very determined.

OLIVIA CLARKE: I joined the local church choir in Mill Hill when I was six and was playing the violin and piano at school. The director of music at church decided to teach me music theory and it must have been a challenge. I was very naughty and would run around the room screaming and then sit down and do a bit of composition when I felt like it. I took grade 5 theory when I was seven in a huge hall at Mill Hill School full of teenage boys. I joined the Finchley Children's Music Group and by eleven I was singing child roles at English National Opera and the Royal Opera House.

BEN GLASSBERG: I was very lucky. I went to a school (Mill Hill School) with excellent music and the Junior

Department of the Royal Academy of Music. From very young I was playing in orchestras and was a percussionist in the National Children's Orchestra.

JONATHON HEYWARD: I grew up in Charleston, South Carolina. I didn't pick up music until quite late and none of my family are musicians. I tried singing, which didn't go well, and my mother strongly encouraged me to try something else. When I was about ten, I went to a school with a free music programme. I signed up for cello and fell in love with it immediately. I was not a sports person at all, so this was such a great outlet for something other than academic work.

Catching the Bug

The desire to be the one at the front, cajoling the musicians, directing, shaping and controlling the music can be something that develops naturally out of these teenage experiences. It can quite simply be born out of a need for someone to take the lead and make it happen, or to help out when the main leader is busy elsewhere. Far from turning paid adult work into free child labour, this is a generous act on the part of teachers and mentors who spot and nurture talent. They are the seed sowers.

SIAN EDWARDS: It was a very gradual and natural progression. I didn't think of myself as a conductor at all in those days. I was in demand as a horn player with various youth orchestras. Often the strings were less competent, so the conductors would ask me to run through the brass and wind music while they rehearsed the strings. It was my status as a horn player that gave me that role and allowed me to spend an hour in front of people. At school they had at least four school orchestras and there were still children who didn't get into those, especially wind players. I was asked to put together a band for them. I arranged some Glenn Miller for four flutes, one oboe, one saxophone, and a few strings. For those who could play only the note C on the flute, then they got to play it as it went past. I conducted them, of course. It was a natural thing to do.

I was inspired by my friends who put on concerts, and out of this was born the Oxford Music Group. It was all part of this tapestry of wonderful music-making in and around Oxford. At seventeen, I hired a church for a very modest fee, and put on a concert with friends, choosing Mozart's 'Prague' Symphony because it doesn't have a minuet and I didn't know how to conduct a minuet!

RICHARD BAKER: Sometimes at choir school we were given a chance to conduct the choir in small pieces, so I did a little then. But at secondary school I started writing music for ambitious productions of plays like *Agamemnon* and *The Crucible* and it was expected that I'd conduct too. It just happened naturally.

HELEN HARRISON: I had done some informal conducting at school, especially with choirs and for shows. I'd often be the one organising the musicians to play, and I'd direct from the piano. I was leader of the Lancashire County Youth Orchestra, and we had a concert in Chorley Town Hall. We were playing Shostakovich's *Festive Overture*, and in the rehearsal the conductor wanted to see what the balance was like in the hall. He asked me to start it, and that was the moment. It was so exciting, and I just loved it.

EÍMEAR NOONE: I started assisting my music teacher in local shows, sometimes playing flute, sometimes piano, leading rehearsals. I always remember her advice: 'If the set falls down, keep vamping!' A lesson for life really.

OLIVIA CLARKE: The choir director encouraged me to take a leadership position in the choir, and, from the age of twelve, it was quite normal for me to take sections of the rehearsal or do the warm-up.

JONATHON HEYWARD: We had a concert at school, and our teacher was ill. The supply teacher knew nothing about music, but someone had to get us through. So we all literally put our names in a hat, shuffled them around, and it was my name that came out. A very shy twelve-year-old, I was terrified, but my curiosity took over. I remember looking at the score, and seeing five lines instead of one, and I wanted to know more. That has always been what fascinates me about conducting – the idea of making something greater than one person. So I decided there and then that I wanted to be a conductor. Once my teacher knew I was interested in conducting, she let me rehearse once a week, and gave me a piece in each concert. I am completely indebted to her for that comfortable feeling I had on the podium from all that experience in my teens.

TIANYI LU: I was nineteen and I wrote a piece for my high school orchestra for a festival and my former music teacher said, 'You wrote it, so why don't you conduct it?' He gave me the very basics (how to beat in three and four), and I did some crazy seagull conducting with lots of enthusiasm but with no clue. We won a gold award. I felt so comfortable on the podium, like a fish in water, but I didn't consider it as a career, nor even see myself as a conductor until later. I was a composer who conducted because someone had to do it.

I too had a teacher who tried to nurture this in me. Graham Garton saw way before I could that my talents might lie in conducting. He patiently took my criticism, when I'd expressed my frustration at the end of choir practice if the tempo in a piece had been unsteady, or when we were singing flat. Without a trace of sarcasm, he would suggest I had a go at improving it, but for reasons I couldn't articulate, I point blank refused. Eventually he persuaded me to start a madrigal group, which I did extremely reluctantly, and the reluctance rubbed off on the singers (my poor friends), so the group didn't last long. I just wasn't ready at that point, but I am so grateful he never told me this was a job only for men, which was the story of so many of my female contemporaries around the world. He had sown seeds, but they were buried very deep.

4: Preparation
to Performance

Not the Whole Story

Back in the early noughties there was a brilliantly entertaining series on Channel 4 called *Faking It*. In each episode a volunteer was given four weeks to learn enough of a new skill to see if they could fool a panel of experts as they performed alongside two or three 'real things'. A vicar tried his hand as a used-car dealer, a sheep shearer as a hairdresser, a ballet dancer as a wrestler. Not all professions can be faked – butcher to surgeon was not on the list. However, a charismatic punk rocker fooled the panel as a conductor. He performed in an informal concert alongside a few young conductors-in-the-making, who were clearly talented and had a lot going on in their heads and were doing things correctly if reservedly with their hands. Innately musical, well tutored but less hampered by all that knowledge and classical music training, the punk rocker got closer to the heart of the music. However, as I defensively pointed out to anyone who would listen, he could fake only the concert part. It's uncomfortable for anyone whose profession can be seemingly so easily faked, and it's easy to dismiss such programmes as superficial and silly, but I was fascinated by the results of this experiment, and it influenced the way I approached teaching.

Anyone with a decent sense of rhythm could learn a series of prepared gestures, yet thinking on your feet, reacting to what comes at you, knowing what to say and do in response, to make things work better – that involves infinite layers of skill, knowledge and preparation. It takes years, even decades of study and experience to master this, but from the start uninhibited physical communication is important, and that is hard for many classical musicians.

Score Preparation

I think this is the hardest, loneliest and most time-consuming part of the job, and the part that no one sees. There's a lot of information that must be fully absorbed before day one of rehearsals. The score, even in quite straightforward music, contains a lot of information.

In printed music, a solo-lined instrument will have one line (stave) to follow. A pianist will have two staves to read simultaneously – right hand on top and left hand below. The music goes along in parallel. The organist has three staves – right hand, left hand and feet, which is an extra bass line.

The conductor works from a full score, and this contains every individual line that every instrument or group of instruments plays. A conductor will read simultaneously anything from five staves in a strings-only piece to upwards of twenty in a large symphonic work. With an opera, there could be multiple choruses (representing different groups of people), all the soloists, and an offstage band as well as

In Good Hands

Excerpt from a full score of Verdi's *Aïda* – Act II Finale. On one page with thirty-three staves, these four bars take barely ten seconds to perform.

62

a pit orchestra, for which you can add another ten or more staves. Some scores are large and heavy, the print often needs to be small, and sometimes only a few bars can be fitted onto one page.

Most middle-aged conductors and orchestral players have an additional handicap – reading long and short distances simultaneously. Reading glasses are great for score study, but they won't work in rehearsal because you need to look up at the whole group as well as read the notes. Varifocal glasses work to an extent, but I don't like conducting with glasses. I think a conductor's eyes are important for communication, and the frames block some peripheral vision, especially in a dark theatre pit. I wear multifocal contact lenses and constantly adjust the prescription to make them work for long and short distances. For the conductor, once they get to the concert, close reading isn't so important because the score is just a quick aide-memoire. That should be true of rehearsals too, but unless you are blessed with a photographic memory you will at least need to tell the orchestra which bar numbers you're talking about, and those numbers are usually *tiny*.

Even with 20/20 vision, a conductor who hasn't prepared will find their head is so deeply buried in the score that they will never be able to dig themselves out and will surely be buried alive by a discerning orchestra.

Orchestral players, particularly section leaders, will have worked on their parts before the rehearsal to a greater or lesser degree. The days and even the night before, they may well have been performing something completely different.

Experienced players may have played the repertoire before. They will also be practising their instruments between rehearsals, so it's not that they work only in rehearsals and performances. They will arrive at the rehearsal ready to work together to shape a performance. They will assume, however, that the conductor comes knowing the score extremely well. That's what they are paid to do.

SIAN EDWARDS: The exhausting part of learning a score is that we are imagining the sounds represented by little black dots on the page into a three-dimensional sound image that's not static. This requires enormous amounts of brainpower.

Score preparation is very personal. Some can absorb scores incredibly fast. I find I take longer than I used to, and certainly the process is more exhausting and intense – I like to think because I understand how to do it better. Ideally you should have the score pretty much from memory. I'm much faster at the early preparation and I have a quick system for breaking down the basics, although it depends partly on the type of work.

For a symphony I make maps of the overall structures, which are formal and familiar. I play it at the piano to hear the harmonies. This is quite straightforward with a Mozart or even a Beethoven score, but with later Romantic works with huge forces this can be torturous. There are some that can whizz through this, but not me. Transposing instruments – written in one key, but sounding in another – are always something to check. For example, when the horn 'in F' has a 'C' on the page, the note will sound as an 'F'. Sometimes they change during the piece – to 'C' or 'E flat'. In some works, on one page of the score you might be looking at clarinets 'in A', cor anglais in F, horns in F *and* in E flat, and trumpets in B flat, all playing simultaneously. So, breaking down the score is important, transposing where necessary and really knowing what every instrument plays. Otherwise the conductor won't understand the harmonies, when someone is playing a wrong note, or when there's a misprint in their part. Some conductors are brilliant instrumentalists but not pianists, and they might not use the piano at all. That's no bad thing, and I have often had to learn scores when I've not had access to a piano. Then you must rely more on your inner ear – looking at the score and imagining the sound. This is a very good discipline. I listen to many different recordings, which is so easy today. In my twenties and early thirties it meant trips to the library, borrowing from friends, or buying expensive CDs. It's a bad idea to try to learn a piece just from listening to recordings. If you listen to only one recording, then you limit your imagination and won't allow your own interpretation, but it never hurts to be exposed to different versions. Later in the learning process, once my own interpretation is growing and I can hear it all in my head, I find it annoying to listen to recordings.

I play through every instrumental line, partly to make sure there are no misprints in the score, and I make special notes of unusual phrase lengths. I mark the dynamics (loud or soft) and expression marks, and the tempo and time signature changes. The blue and red pencil is my (and many of my colleagues') best friend. You can buy the half-red half-blue pencil in specialist art shops in Europe, but strangely not in the UK. I use the blue end for cueing instruments, and the red for dynamics. I know some conductors who use them for dynamics only: red for *forte* and *crescendo*, and blue for *piano* and *diminuendo*. Some people are snobbish about colours, and don't approve of overmarking a score, but this is a very personal thing, and whatever it takes to get there is surely the priority. I then go back to look at the structure in greater detail, following the harmonic progressions and how the composer has built up the textures. I work out how to conduct it – how I would wave my hands around to make it work. There are some bits of score learning I can do in a cafe or library, but the waving, perhaps not.

Because I learn the scores more thoroughly now, it takes more for me to trust I know them properly. The bit that takes the longest is imagination, really bringing a score to life. I liken it to studying for an exam. With a bit of revision and knowledge and an ability to wing it, you might scrape by. If you memorise a lot of the information, that will certainly raise your grade. But really knowing your subject in depth takes it to another level and that leaves you feeling you could always do more preparation. Depending on the complexity of the piece, a conductor can probably read a score through once, have a fairly good idea of how it might sound, even conduct it with an orchestra at a basic level, but that's not good enough to lead a group. A conductor might seem to get away with a superficial knowledge of the score, but it will make for a dull rehearsal and performance. Sometimes, for a last-minute concert engagement, or when they have so many different projects going on that their time is limited, they will have to use their experience and knowledge to speed learn a work.

Learning scores often happens while other projects are in rehearsal. This can mean late nights, early mornings, and might be a reason why conductors seem a bit grumpy sometimes. Again, time management is crucial.

MARIN ALSOP: I like to do a lot of harmonic, structural and dynamic analysis, but the most important thing for me is finding the narrative. There are basics to studying a score, but it is also important to work out your own style of study, and the style must suit the person.

ANTONIO PAPPANO: The conductor's job is to create a hierarchy of importance. The tune is easier to hear, but the harmonic progression is where the journey really takes place. You must know the role of each section of the orchestra at any given moment. A score isn't solid. It needs to be broken down to its component parts, and then to be fitted all together again, encompassing all the facets that you think will tell the story. You work out who's going to need you and often it's the accompaniment rather than the melody. I work in detail, but I also sit at the piano and play through the whole thing, so that I don't always get bogged down in that detail. Eventually I find I have everything, or my version of everything. I still believe it's a kind of miracle that it all comes together in a performance.

Rehearsals

Good hands are very important, particularly when rehearsal time is limited. Orchestras don't like conductors who talk too much, or who say one thing but then show something completely different with their hands. But words *are* important. Perhaps because the baton technique is the only bit the audience sees, it's all too easy to believe this is how the magic is woven. So much has been written about conductors and their gestures that young conductors can fall into the trap of thinking that's all they need to develop.

Depending on the country or the orchestra, the rehearsal period for a symphonic concert can be anything from three hours on the day to six hours every day for a week. The UK is famous for having some of the best sight-readers in the world, reproducing the notes on the page at first glance with almost no errors. This has come about through a culture of managing with as little rehearsal as possible, and time is money. There are full-time salaried players in some UK orchestras, but it's much more common in Europe where they tend to have more state support, and can afford longer rehearsals with more breaks. This can make for differing rehearsing cultures. The conductor should be sensitive to this, and manage their time extremely well, so the musicians are neither bored nor stressed for the concert itself.

At the start of the first rehearsal, it's best to allow the orchestra to play. Every conductor I've interviewed has said the same thing. That they start with a short greeting, then they play for at least five to ten minutes before going back to rehearse in detail, so orchestra and conductor can settle. Then they need to know what to fix technically, what sounded wrong, and what will fix itself by repetition. The musicians will be making fast mental notes of what they need to correct, and a conductor that points all this out without giving them a chance to correct mistakes themselves is seen as a bit rude, annoying, bullying, stupid or inexperienced. Yet, since we are dealing with a large group of people, no matter how brilliant they are as individuals, some things will need to be fixed by the conductor.

For example, if there is a problem with intonation (when instruments are not in tune with each other), in a professional orchestra this can usually be resolved by the players themselves. Sometimes a conductor must intervene, but it is a delicate balance. The players will often know what needs to be done and pointing it out early on can be annoying for those involved, and that type of overcriticism can stress players and make intonation even worse.

BRAMWELL TOVEY: Sometimes you just have to say directly if it's sharp or flat, but it can be done in a non-challenging way, using succinct, non-threatening language.

People know when they get it wrong, and if they have any doubts about what they are doing, then the last thing they need is for it to be pointed out to the whole room. But at times you need to say something, and these things can be fixed without it being controversial.

The notes on the page give a huge amount of information and trying to achieve all of that is hard enough, but there are still many ways of realising those notes – subtle changes in tempo, bringing out contrasting colours, instruments, changes in dynamics, and overall pacing. And every member of the orchestra will probably have their own views on how the music could go, especially if it's a work they have played many times before. They could have individual ideas, or perhaps the orchestra has recently played the work with a different conductor. Another work might be completely new to the players, and since they have only one line of music to read, the conductor helps tie these strands together to make a coherent whole. The conductor will attempt simultaneously to react to what comes at them from the orchestra, so as not to stick rigidly to something that's not working, but also to steer a clear and decisive path.

Essential to this is a good pair of ears. The conductor should be listening so acutely that they can quickly spot the wrong notes or bad ensemble and correct them where necessary, but ideally they should start making and shaping music too. If they just focus on correcting, it can make for a boring and uninspiring rehearsal.

Conductors often use their voices not just for speaking but to sing. All musicians can sing. Not many conductors are trained singers, and it doesn't need to sound pretty (mine certainly doesn't) but singing a phrase can portray just what they want with far more immediacy than a long-winded verbal description.

It might be that a conductor's gestures are hampering the process, however impressive they might look, and that could well be the reason for ensemble problems and even wrong notes. If a conductor doesn't develop healthy self-criticism, they will never allow an orchestra to fulfil its potential. Blaming an orchestra for bad ensemble or an irregular tempo can be deeply demoralising and stressful for players, who will probably know that the problem doesn't lie with them.

There are also subtler ways a conductor will affect the sound if their body isn't giving concise information. A tense conductor is more likely to make a tense sound. I believe that humility and self-awareness are essential for a good conductor, and these should be lifelong challenges. Bad habits can sneak in for all conductors, no matter how technically proficient they were when they came out of college. When a conductor is still training and taking masterclasses, then other conductors (their teachers and peers) will be critiquing their gestures all the time, and they should have learned to be their own critic as well. But there soon comes a time when that network disappears, and they are on their own. In some ways that's very good because it allows the conductor to develop their own voice, but everyone has technical weaknesses that they might have ironed out early on. As with all bad habits, if you're not careful, they will creep back.

ANTONIO PAPPANO: I work on my baton technique, which I've never felt was my strong point. I work on breathing and getting less involved with my breath in the passion of the music, because I find it can lock my body. My beats become shorter, and the fluidity is impeded. I work even on basic things, where is the three, where is the four, is my shoulder stiff, is it free, am I centred? The ABC basically. That is something I personally need to do. There are some who just have it naturally with no problems, but I am constantly aware.

BARRY WORDSWORTH: There are two reasons why you need to make sure your technique is working. Firstly, so that your musicians are not put off by what you're doing, and that it helps them. The second is so you don't do yourself any damage. Conducting is physically hard work, especially operas and ballets, which are seldom under three hours. It's marvellous cardiovascular work, but when I went back to conducting after the pandemic, I started doing Pilates as part of my preparation. Otherwise, it would have been a shock to my body.

I've recently bought an Apple Watch, and one minute into rehearsing a particularly energetic piece, it vibrated with a message: 'You seem to be doing an indoor run. Would you like to record the exercise?' On the first day of stage rehearsals with full orchestra and cast of the one-hour, one-act opera *Gianni Schicchi* by Puccini, we did four run-throughs. In the first run-through the orchestra was too loud for singers in places, and I noticed when looking at my 'health data' that I burned more calories than later in the day when the balance was better. My gestures had probably been too big.

To keep their technique in check, it's a really good idea for conductors of any age to watch video footage of themselves, all the way through their careers. I found this particularly useful in a run of performances of Ravel's *La Valse*. I knew I was technically clear because the ensemble was good, but it was lacking something. The lush impressionistic sound of the interwoven Viennese waltzes just wasn't there, and nor was the dramatic arc of the piece as the tension builds to an eventual musical explosion and controlled destruction. After seeing gestures (especially with my left hand) I wouldn't advise my students to do, I was able to improve in each performance, and get back on track. I think the final performance sounded better.

Another essential factor is time management. Every bit of music must be rehearsed. Some sections might be harder than others, and some bits might be so hard that it's tempting to focus too much on them and run out of time.

Conductors Are Human Too

Rehearsals are the test for the conductor because in some

ways they are giving a performance to the orchestra, especially if it's a group new to them. Most conductors I interviewed admitted to feeling more nervous in rehearsal than in performance. When an orchestra works with a new conductor the players normally feed back to the management. Some orchestras have a greater say than others in who they get to work with, but their opinions are rarely completely ignored. It's rare for every member of the orchestra to share the same opinion, but there's often a general feeling. The rehearsal is the test, and the first rehearsal can be 'make or break', even for experienced well-known conductors. It's often said that an orchestra will decide whether they like you, not just in the first rehearsal, or even the first hour of a rehearsal, but before you start conducting. The minute you stand on that podium. It might be a slight exaggeration, but there's no doubting it's much harder to get an orchestra back on side if you lose them early on.

With so much at stake, there can be demons at play who try to shift our focus away from the music. Bramwell Tovey was to conduct his debut subscription concert with the New York Philharmonic in 2000. This is one of the most prestigious orchestras in the world and they work with some of the great names in the business.

About a month before the rehearsal, I started to become paralysed with nerves. I was picked up at the airport by Lorin Maazel's personal chauffeur, and he said, 'Oh yes! I just dropped off Kurt Masur . . . and Lorin Maazel was in here the other day.' I felt like a fraud. He took me to the Mayflower Hotel on Central Park and said, 'I'll pick you up in the morning, maestro. It's only two blocks, but I'm to take you over.' So, the next day I was in the dressing room, and there's Mahler's score of this and Toscanini's score of that, and the original flute part of Dvořák's 'New World' Symphony. I look out of the window and there's Alice Tully Hall, the Juilliard School and I can hear the New York Philharmonic warming up. And all I'm thinking is, 'I have to get out of here!'

The personnel manager walked me to the rehearsal room and said, 'I have to make some announcements. Will you stand at the side of the stage, and then I'll bring you on?' So, while he was talking, I spotted the exit door about five feet away. I had brought my coat and case with me because I was intending to leave the building. I was a bag of nerves.

Then the oboist played the A, and everything just went calm. I thought, 'What's the matter with me? I can do this.' So, I walked out there, everything lifted off me, I did my rehearsal, and I felt amazing. But I had been within five seconds of running. I believe that in that arc of time, there's something very crucial that transforms us from being just someone with the scores under our arm to being the conductor on the podium. But there's a certain rite of passage, and of course you can analyse it in different ways. But it was the oboe A that saved me and provided me with the way forward.

When I understood it was all about the music and not

the famous orchestra, it was fine. I was so obsessed with thoughts like 'Kurt Masur's bottom has been on this seat, and Lorin Maazel's bottom on this seat. And this is the driver who has taken around Zubin Mehta and Leonard Bernstein and now it's me. What am I doing here?

Since then, I've had a much healthier attitude to everything. It was almost as if I thought, 'I am the little boy, who had come from the Salvation Army brass band in Ilford, whose dad died, and whose mum was a single parent. Here I am at the New York Philharmonic.' I felt like a fraud. It's so stupid. A monument to my own stupidity.

It's about getting rid of all the dross that can weigh us down. Now I'm sixty-seven years old, and I've got cancer. Most places I go, the orchestra knows I've had cancer. There's tremendous sympathy, people are generous, and I'm liked, which is nice. I can enjoy myself. If I were to go somewhere and not be respected, I'd just leave. I don't care anymore. But it's taken me forty-five years to get to this place *and* having cancer. It's the only good thing about having cancer.

The fact that these men, these great maestros had intimidated Bramwell, even in their absence, shows the godlike power that we give them.

Is a certain level of nerves necessary and normal? Is it healthy? Well, yes, I think it probably is, so long as those moments are rare, and the payback is much greater. I'd go as far as to say there should always be a bit of nerves in the mix, because it means the conductor still cares passionately about the music and their fellow artists. Most performers will get nervous sometimes, especially in new situations – performing a new work for the first time, or working with a new company, and that is likely to continue throughout their careers. That is no less true of conductors just because they are ostensibly in charge.

ANTONIO PAPPANO: I can get nervous in front of the Royal Opera House orchestra when I haven't conducted there for a bit. When you're in front of a big orchestra, even one you have a long relationship with, it's about the respect for them, and honouring the demands of the music. The only thing that gets me out of that state of imposter syndrome is to study more.

In 2013 Jane Glover made her Metropolitan Opera debut conducting *Die Zauberflöte*.

At my first rehearsal with the orchestra, I think I was as scared as I have ever been for anything. I did a bit of the overture, stopped, and worked on the balance of the brass chords. I got this feeling that everyone was thinking, 'OK, yes, she knows what she's doing.' Then I let them play and stopped to correct a few things, and by the break in the rehearsal I was feeling fine, and they were lovely, welcoming and supportive.

It is comforting for all of us to hear these human stories from conductors with so much experience, reputation and success. I know that initial feeling, that sense of foreboding before a first rehearsal will never go away, and just knowing that calms me down somehow. Over the years I have come to recognise it as an old tiresome acquaintance that I've learned to tolerate. Sometimes it can be a good friend, reminding me to work hard and avoid complacency. I try not to allow it to creep in unnoticed and chip away at my confidence, nor do I let it hang around too long and become a distraction, an irritation or sometimes even a saboteur. It's nowhere to be seen after a decent performance or rehearsal, and every performer's best friend, the 'post-performance high', dominates that moment. But in the days and weeks that follow it can reappear and start questioning, niggling away at things that might not have gone so well. Again, that can be useful, a critical friend, but it needs keeping in check if it's not to dominate.

For young conductors very early in their careers, the challenges are immense, because on the podium they are supposedly in charge, but they are often in a junior/apprenticeship role, sometimes assisting very famous and brilliant conductors. It wasn't until I started to be engaged as a 'first' conductor/music director on an opera that I realised how much easier this was than assisting. Yes, there was more responsibility, but once the first rehearsal is done, the length of the rehearsal process allows the music director to establish themselves and gain trust. Time constraints prevent a 'second'/assistant conductor from having any meaningful rehearsal time with the orchestra. There's often an opportunity and need to build up a relationship with the singers, and sometimes an assistant might rehearse the singers in advance of the main conductor arriving. This will really help when jumping in on a performance, but unless the first conductor is terrible, then it is always a tough gig.

> JANE GLOVER: Way back when I was assisting Bernard Haitink on *Don Giovanni* at Glyndebourne, I was given six performances, after he had conducted the first eight. He got rave reviews of course and my first thought was, 'All I can possibly do is make this worse.' But taking over shows is a great way to learn.

When I was training, while there were many kind and thoughtful friends among my fellow conducting students, we really didn't talk about nerves, behaviour and showing vulnerability. Twenty or thirty years ago, particularly in Russia, the old style of leadership was the norm, and no one thought to challenge it. 'Never admit to a mistake, and never show weakness.' I knew it could be more nuanced than that, as I had observed some great conductors be kind, gentle, and even put their hand up to mistakes in rehearsals, but there were plenty of truly terrifying maestros up there too. I felt I had no choice but to be myself, and instinctively I knew that putting on an act wouldn't work, but I had no one with whom to thrash out these ideas. The lack of female role models didn't help.

I am heartened by the upcoming generation. From many I have spoken to in recent years, male and female, they have an impressive sophistication and maturity. A wider variety of conductor personalities is emerging, and they are questioning and challenging the status quo.

TIANYI LU: I think a focus on wellbeing is missing in a lot of conducting training and music generally. Not that long ago, it was even taboo to talk about RSI for instrumentalists, and now I think it's important to focus also on mental health and psychology. Whenever I am invited to speak or teach, I always like creating the space for these discussions as it is a huge part of navigating a career.

OLIVIA CLARKE: I am chronically shy and an introvert, and as a child I felt much more comfortable with adults. I have a performing self which I present to people. It is sincere, and it is me, but it is draining, and I need down time to recover.

The climate is shifting, and this is making older conductors, teachers and mentors less guarded. As a result, I see a new generation that is more resilient, less insecure and defensive, and therefore less aggressive.

JONATHON HEYWARD: Having open talks with experienced conductors has really helped, and that knowledge can be incredibly empowering for a young conductor. I know that nerves won't ever entirely go away, but I can use them to my advantage instead of letting them stifle me.

As a cellist I had such terrible nerves I would freeze on stage. I wanted to address this at the Boston Conservatoire, so started taking Alexander Technique lessons, and both physically and mentally it was a door-opener.

As a conductor I try to go back to the naivety I had as the fourteen-year-old – to return to why I wanted to do this. More recently I decided to learn meditation and mindfulness practice which is something I now do daily – mixed in with Alexander Technique. As conductors we are constantly thinking about other things that have nothing to do with the music. So being able to focus everything back down to the music in front of you is essential.

BEN GLASSBERG: When I was a teenager and determined to become a conductor, and as a student, it never crossed my mind to think I might be an imposter. My nerves came later as I became more successful. The first rehearsal is always so hard; even with a group who know me quite well now, I think, 'Today they are going to realise I'm not good at this.' I conducted a concert recently with a new orchestra and the first hour was tough. I felt I was undergoing a subconscious test, but after that they were lovely.

Ben and Jonathon are both former students of Sian Edwards who is full of pearls of wisdom. It's very rare for a conductor to meet any of the players in advance of the first rehearsal. It is a heightened moment: as they stand by the podium, the orchestra is warming up, then the manager introduces the conductor, perhaps giving a few notices first – that moment when Bramwell so nearly ran away.

SIAN EDWARDS: Before the rehearsal starts, look around at the players as they are warming up their instruments and tuning. You will see that some of them naturally look quite serious when playing. Noticing this can help when later you say something to them, and it seems that their serious expression means they don't like your idea, or they think you're an idiot. Of course, this could be the case, but you could also remind yourself that it's just their natural professional concentration making them look stern, and it's not personal.

My concentrating face is also somewhat grumpy, and I make sure I don't inadvertently direct that at some poor player who might think I have it in for them. My smile is better than my frown, though very occasionally the latter is useful.

Bramwell had similar advice: 'As I am being introduced, this is my chance to study the room. It's good to observe rather than simply be observed.'

Humour

Creating the right atmosphere in the room to achieve all that needs to be done in a rehearsal is largely down to the conductor. Some conductors use humour and, sad to say, a few are rude and bullying, but happily that that's much rarer and not so tolerated these days. I use humour a lot in everyday life to connect with people, so it makes sense I would use it in rehearsals.

MARIN ALSOP: Humour is my 'go to', and I think everybody has different methods of coping and finding a way of making that connection with the orchestra initially. But you can't use it all the time. Earlier in my career I used it more, but then a colleague in the orchestra told me, 'The orchestra likes and respects you. You don't have to be funny.' But it is a great way of putting people at ease and creating a good atmosphere.

BRAMWELL TOVEY: When I was a teenager and becoming really interested in conducting, I read a lot about [Thomas] Beecham, [John] Barbirolli and [Malcolm] Sargent. I thought Beecham's much celebrated humour was cruel and bullying and not very clever, but I did like the idea of humour. With a well-chosen line, a quick thought, you can prick a balloon, and dispel a situation, just like a diplomat. I had two very good friends from my grammar school, and we all shared our experiences of negotiating a roomful of public-school boys who seemed so confident and entitled. Humour could help with that. Then I noticed that orchestras would start listening to me if they thought

I was going to say something amusing. It was a way of getting them quiet. So initially I used it quite mechanically, but these days it's more natural. If I say something early on that makes them smile, it levels the playing field.

ANTONIO PAPPANO: Humour is very personal and is a useful tool. You don't have to be a stand-up comedian, but it's just how you say something in passing or how you react to someone playing a wrong note. A smile can help, but I am the first to admit that I have shot deadly glances when I'm unhappy. You need a very good reason to explode. The clichéd view of the conductor as a grey-haired demi-monster with ultimate authority is passé.

BARRY WORDSWORTH: There's the famous story about Sir Adrian [Boult] inviting Toscanini to conduct the BBC Symphony Orchestra for the first time. Toscanini complained they weren't playing in time, so he got out his pocket watch, threw it on the floor and stamped on it. The concert went very well, and afterwards the orchestra gave him a new watch they had clubbed together to buy him. I think that sort of childish behaviour on his part wouldn't be tolerated or even seen as funny these days, and that's a good thing.

I remember Sir Adrian saying to me, 'Just remember, you're a first amongst equals. You're there to do what the orchestra cannot do itself.'

JANE GLOVER: It's possible to be collegial as a conductor. I love suggestions from players, and that becomes easier when you know it's coming from a place of respect. It's much harder for young conductors. Eye contact is very important too, especially in the first rehearsal where you make that human contact with them.

Performance

If the preparation and rehearsals have gone well, then the chances are the performance will too. In many ways this is the least stressful and most enjoyable part of the job. But beware conductors who enjoy themselves too much! There's still so much work to be done – listening, leading, reacting, inspiring, and most importantly that extra something to elevate it from rehearsal to performance. Orchestras might forgive or even relish a slightly faster tempo here and there, but big surprises and inconsistences are unwelcome.

ANTONIO PAPPANO: Orchestras can play pretty well on their own, and so what is the conductor there for? Score preparation, rehearsal technique, but also to suggest, to spur on, to encourage that which is going to make the music not only palatable, but fresh and alive to the listener. Often playing music that people have heard a hundred times before. So why listen to that hundred and first time? The conductor is a cheerleader, the encourager in chief, if you like. It sounds a bit corny, but it is crucial.

In Good Hands

These days, thanks to the likes of Leonard Bernstein and later Marin Alsop, conductors are turning round and speaking to their audiences. I think this is a good thing in many settings, though it is a challenge for some. Conductors are used to communicating with their people – their fellow musicians – but the public is a different thing. Some have a professorial tendency to lecture, which can be perfect for some audiences, but off-putting and intimidating for others. Pitching it right is hard. Others just don't enjoy it and would much rather focus on the music and nothing else. That is completely understandable, and addressing the audience is not for all. But it can help in breaking down barriers between the audience and orchestra, providing a welcoming environment to people who might think classical music is stuffy.

The concert is the front-facing part of our job, despite the fact we have our backs to the audience for most of it. It's useful for conducting students to listen to conductors' different interpretations so they don't become too seduced by the beauty of their gestures alone. The gestures might be incredible, but what does the orchestra actually sound like? For an audience there's no getting away from the conductor. The conductor is bang in the centre, standing up, unlike the rest of the orchestra, and unless you have a bad seat or close your eyes, they are hard to ignore. Unless the conductor is entirely lacking in personality and ability, they will influence the orchestral sound in a concert for good or bad. Do a conductor's movements influence the ears of an audience? I think we would be wrong if we believed they made no difference at all. They can help make sense of the music for the audience, or indeed disturb and confuse them.

5: Training

Which Route?

How do you learn all these skills? Do you take exams? Are there competitions?

There is no one route to becoming a conductor. It's not like training to be a doctor, where passing exams and work experience take you to the next level at every stage of your career, and where, if you have relevant qualifications, you can pretty much guarantee you will find a job somewhere. Some conductors have two or three degrees even to doctoral level; others have very little formal conducting training, and have gained experience through entrepreneurial means such as starting their own orchestras. Despite the time and financial investment both entail (and this is sadly not available to everyone), it will not guarantee employment or a long career. Others train as an apprentice in an opera house, learning on the job and rising through the ranks. This has the benefit of financial security, but some people find themselves stuck at one stage of their career and can get pigeonholed, particularly if their personal life won't allow them to move to a new theatre or even a new country where there could be more opportunities.

University

Conductors will have studied at least one instrument to a high level. Most will have a bachelor's degree in Music either at university, where the focus might be more on musicology, or at a conservatoire, where they receive a more practical training in an instrument. If they come to conducting slightly later, they could also have a master's degree in an instrument, singing, composition or musicology. A few start with a degree in another subject altogether, but they will have kept making music at a high level throughout. It is rarer these days and is more common in the UK, where a degree in any subject from a leading university might simply be seen as proof you have a brain and a capacity to learn, and the extra-curricular achievements are more relevant.

So, continuing with my Classics degree might not have prevented me from becoming a conductor, though I am mightily glad I changed to music. Although the music degree at Oxford was a little dry and academic, it was a useful grounding for a conductor. Being able to write in the style of Palestrina, Bach, Mozart and Beethoven, learning how to rearrange a piano work for a full orchestra, reading a full score at the piano, analysis of scores and an in-depth study of the history of Western classical music all helped. There was a bit too much emphasis on early music for my taste, and not quite enough practical music, but there were other opportunities for that. My tutor, John Warrack, not only had extraordinary insights into Classical and Romantic music and its place in wider history but, unlike some, he loved music. I continued to take organ lessons in London; my organ-scholar duties gave me hands-on conducting experience, and I was busy playing the trumpet in ensembles and orchestras around town.

John also gave me some very good advice in my final year, as my focus turned to conducting. I was worried that running St Hugh's Music Society would impact on my academic work. While giving it up was the last thing I wanted to do, I voiced my concerns. John was practical, wise and refreshingly unconventional for a person in charge of my academic development:

> My dear Alice, you're definitely not heading for a first-class degree [something only a very few achieved back then], but you'll get some kind of second come what may, and it doesn't really matter that much whether it's high or low. I can see conducting is something you really love, and when you leave here you are going to need more than a degree on your C.V. to make any impact. Keep up with the conducting.

Jane Glover made a similar decision when she conducted *Le nozze di Figaro* in her final term: 'Conducting *Figaro* taught me more than my entire Oxford education.'

She is also an alumna of St Hugh's and I love the fact that the Mordan Hall (a fusty mahogany-panelled room, looking like something straight out of a Dorothy L. Sayers novel) was the venue for both of us in our first conducting attempts. Jane's academic achievements are in a completely different league from mine. She stayed on in Oxford for doctoral studies in seventeenth-century Venetian opera, and her tutor, Frederick Sternfeld, had a sparkling academic career mapped out for her.

> JANE GLOVER: I felt it was more important for me to perform music than to write about it, and I don't think Fred ever forgave me for my decision to move away from academia.

Yet Jane's extraordinary abilities and drive enabled her to do both to the very highest standards, and that is a rare achievement.

London

In 1992 I graduated from Oxford – my head full of interesting though not terribly useful knowledge when it came to surviving in the adult world. All I had was a strong yet vague idea I wanted to conduct more. I would hope Oxford University Careers Centre has improved since the 1990s but in those days, it was useful only if you wanted a well-paid city job, to continue in university academia or to become a schoolteacher. None of those appealed. What on earth was I going to do?

The only things I could do quite well were playing the

organ and basic conducting. There are many churches in London and most require organists. The work is rarely well paid, but it does sometimes include accommodation. I returned to Norfolk in June determined to get to London as soon as possible and trawled the *Church Times* for 'Situations Vacant'. I was lucky and a month later I moved into a small flat in Marylebone beside the church where I was to be organist for the next five years: St Mary's, Bryanston Square. This job was unpaid, but the flat was rent free. My only duties were confined to Sunday mornings and, as I didn't have to find money for expensive London rent, I had time to work on the skills I knew I needed for conducting. I found some part-time piano teaching in schools and worked a few mornings a week as a receptionist for a local osteopath. I think I was bad at both these jobs, and apologies to anyone I half-heartedly tried to teach or anyone whose appointments I forgot to register. My mind was elsewhere.

Not only did I have a roof over my head in smart central London, but I had a ready-made performance venue with a fantastic acoustic. The job itself wasn't particularly taxing and I could have done the minimum, but this was an opportunity for conducting, and *I* needed to make that happen. I arm-twisted and bribed my friends (with beer) to sing some musically ambitious services once a month, and then I formed the Wyndham Chamber Orchestra.

This sounds a lot grander than it was, and consisted of my university friends, most of whom, though very talented musicians, were doing sensible things like training for the law. Some friends from university were taking postgraduate music degrees at London conservatoires, and I inveigled myself into that social network too. This was in the days before email, and mobile phones were extremely expensive both to own and to use. Landline calls were the only option, and not everyone had an answerphone – it wasn't called voicemail in those days. I had a funny little gadget that you could hold to the microphone bit of the handset and punch in a code that allowed you to dial from any phone but using your own BT account. This came in handy during quiet moments at the osteopath's reception. I feel somewhat guilty for keeping the line engaged, but at least I was paying for the calls. It was a very stressful thing to organise but nonetheless I managed to put on three or four concerts a year for a few years, building a small repertoire. Most importantly, I got podium time (a bit like air miles for a pilot).

I had a very good teacher during that period: Neil Thomson, who was Head of Conducting at the Royal College of Music and who gave me an excellent grounding in conducting technique. I also began to find jobs conducting amateur orchestras and choirs around London. Guy's & St Thomas's Hospital was particular fun, especially the after-concert parties. Medics are way better at partying than music students. I also conducted a lawyers' choir, which could become tiresome when they wanted me to justify everything I asked of them. I conducted a small professional choir in a weekday service at St Stephen Walbrook in the City of London – the beautiful Wren domed church where the Samaritans was founded by the maverick priest Chad Varah, who was still incumbent.

I was very keen to get into opera and I have two conductors to thank for welcoming me into this world. The Music Director of University College London, David Drummond, was one of those important people all budding conductors need. I wrote to him cold to ask if there were any assisting opportunities. Unlike most people I wrote to, he replied, met me, and gave me a lot of work, as well as some very good advice in those early years. A position at European Chamber Opera sprung out of that, and for the first time I was assisting a woman – Andrea Quinn. She very generously gave me one of her performances of Mozart's *Die Zauberflöte* at Holland Park Theatre. I had been assisting her throughout the rehearsal process and had done my homework, but I'm glad there's no recorded evidence of it. Everyone needs a first time.

I quickly realised that opera was where I felt most at home. The complex process of bringing together singers, orchestra and stage was a drama in itself, and I loved the immersive nature of six weeks working towards one thing.

Postgraduate Studies

There was no doubt that I required more training. There were gaps in my knowledge and technique, and I felt I needed to be a full-time student again, so I went about applying to conservatoires for postgraduate study. This went disastrously.

Competition for postgraduate conducting study is fierce.

Most conservatoires offer only two or three places a year, and it is difficult for those deciding on who goes through to know just what they are looking for. Raw talent and potential are essential, but that's hard to judge unless the conductors have enough of the right experience to show these qualities. And the audition process allows only a limited time with the orchestra, so confident (one might say flashy) types are going to make the best impression. We know that orchestras make an instant judgement about a conductor, and perhaps that's fair enough for the trained and experienced, but for a conductor-in-the-making I'm not so sure. I can't offer a solution and I know the decisions as to who makes it through are carefully considered.

As well as enjoying a highly successful career in her own right, at the Royal Academy of Music Sian Edwards runs one of the most prestigious courses around. The alumni speak for themselves, immediately going on to win international competitions and assistantships with major orchestras.

SIAN EDWARDS: When I was applying for conducting courses, I didn't see myself as a conductor, but as someone who was going to become a conductor. There were others who had that swagger and called themselves a conductor when they barely had any experience at all. Now, as someone in the position of choosing who goes on some of these courses, I know it's not always possible to spot the one who twenty years down the line will succeed. This year we had seventy-one applicants for the master's course at the

Academy. It took me ages to look through the videos and I kept asking, 'Who are you in there?'

It's also hard when they come from such different backgrounds. Most European countries offer undergraduate conducting courses, and even if they have a degree in an instrument, it's expected that conductors first study for a bachelor's in conducting. In the UK we go straight to a master's, and it's assumed that the first degree, combined with student or amateur conducting experience, will make up that knowledge. Applicants may have taken short courses, conducting electives and private lessons, but their experience is less formal – forming their own groups, conducting their friends. Both backgrounds have their pros and cons.

SIAN EDWARDS: There are some highly trained and gifted musicians who've studied conducting for years, but haven't had to convince a group of people, even if they're friends, how they want the music to sound. They have to develop that urgent and very real need to communicate their ideas and feelings about music. The British way of having a desire for the music and going out there and making it happen can be good; the would-be conductor may have a more individual and inspired idea of what they are trying to do. On the other hand, that British habit of somehow expecting to know how to do it before we're taught how to do it can have its drawbacks.

Back in the early 1990s there was no video submission, though actually I wish there had been, as I had some quite decent footage from my concerts. We were interviewed, given aural tests, and had to play something on our first-study instrument. I did reasonably well at this, though my reticence and lack of awareness of how to project a confident personality meant that I hardly sparkled – likewise when I met the orchestra. It was all over too quickly and was too stressful for me to settle. I spent three years attempting to get a place on a course in different institutions. I usually got very close and was often on waiting lists to replace someone who might drop out, but I never quite made it.

I am not alone in struggling with this. Unbelievably, Jane Glover was refused a place at the Guildhall School of Music & Drama for unclear reasons. Marin Alsop made two attempts to get into the prestigious Juilliard School, and was told her piano playing wasn't good enough. Despite a master's degree from the very same institution, they also questioned her academic qualifications. Marin was an accomplished violinist, which many would argue is more useful than playing the piano well, since she had real experience of playing in orchestras. She eventually gave up on the idea of study, founded her own orchestra and went on to become one of the most successful conductors in the world. She is also Professor and Director of the Graduate Conducting Program at the Peabody Institute in the US.

MARIN ALSOP: I think the key element I'm looking for is the connection to the sound of the orchestra. They must feel that sound and have this physical imagination. I think authenticity and the ability to be themselves, to be present, is so important. And of course, at a very mundane level, if you don't have a fantastic inner rhythm and ear, you shouldn't be a conductor. You can develop it to a certain extent, but you need some gift in that.

Three years in a row I failed to get onto a postgraduate conducting course. 'This would be the moment to go in another direction surely, Alice!' I think many of my friends and family thought. Despite my lack of confidence, there was a fire in my belly and a downright stubbornness that made me refuse to give up. If anything, every failure made me more determined. Stubbornness can be a dangerous thing in a conductor, but I believe it is also essential, and has helped me to overcome the many challenges of this career.

There were musicians whom I respected who continued to encourage me, and I simply didn't allow the nay-sayers in. Perhaps my slow start and my repeat year at school had given me patience and awareness that I just needed to take a bit longer – ever the tortoise, never the hare. Then along came the possibility of Russia and my life changed for ever.

Ilya Alexanzh

I first saw the great pedagogue and conductor Ilya

Alexandrovich Musin giving a masterclass at the Royal Academy of Music in the mid-1990s. Born in tsarist Russia, he shared his decades with the century, and at ninety-one he had been teaching conducting for nearly seventy years. He was a legend in Russia, having taught generations of conductors, yet he was barely known outside the Soviet Union. That was, until Sian Edwards went to study with him in 1983.

SIAN EDWARDS: I was on a conducting course in the summer of 1981 in the Netherlands with Neeme Järvi teaching. He got up to conduct one day, and it was as if someone had turned on the lights in the hall. This beautiful, elegant, wonderful conducting, so kind and inviting the players to make music together. I went up to him afterwards and said, 'How can I learn to conduct like you?' He said, 'You have to study at the Leningrad Conservatoire.'

After my horn studies at the Royal Northern College, I won a scholarship to return there to do a postgraduate diploma in conducting, but I remembered Järvi's words. In those days there wasn't so much teaching of conducting in this country, and my diploma was a strange hybrid course where I was put in front of orchestras, but not given much guidance. Not enough thought had been given to how a young musician can flourish in an institution where they are neither teaching nor an undergraduate, and yet they have some authority and are supposed to know how to do it. People were very happy to criticise: 'Your head moves too much, your elbows are sticking out, you're dancing around the podium.' So, you stop all that, but then have nothing to replace it with.

In the winter of 1982–3, I applied to the British Council to study in St Petersburg, or Leningrad as it was. I waited for months, and nothing happened, so after my final exam in Manchester, I got a job in McDonald's. Then in early September I got a call saying, 'Can you come to the Foreign Office in London next week. We think we might be able to send you to Russia.' In that interview I was told, 'You know that if there's a war, we may not be able to get you out.' I said, 'Well, frankly, if there's a war, it's going to be total destruction anyway, so it won't matter where I am, will it?' That afternoon they told me, 'You are on the list of people who will go to Russia tomorrow morning, for ten months.'

I arrived initially in Moscow and couldn't even say 'hello' in Russian. Luckily there was a returning English historian doing a doctoral thesis who spoke Russian and helped me get to Leningrad. He took me to the student hostel where I was to live for the duration. The lady at the door was terrified initially and thought I was some kind of enemy agent. I arrived on a Sunday, and the linen cupboard was opened only on Tuesdays, so I didn't have any sheets or blankets, but my new Soviet roommate helped me out.

I was allocated to Arvid Jansons as my teacher [father of Mariss Jansons – one of the finest conductors of recent times]. Arvid spoke very good English, but it was Musin who was the most popular professor, and it was very hard to get into his class. I watched him teaching, and one day I blurted out, 'I think I'm going to leave Russia unless I can take lessons with you.' Musin thought it was terrible that this *Anglichanka* (English girl) might leave, so he agreed to let me conduct for him to see what I was like. A wonderful Kazakh friend and fellow conductor, Nurlan Zharasov, helped me prepare for my audition. Musin did agree to take me, despite his wife Anna Aranovna being furious because he had a heart condition and she felt he was doing too much. I realised I must do well to prove my worth.

What struck me instantly in that room at the Academy when I saw Musin teaching was how quickly the student conductors transformed from well-schooled, precise conductors to expressive beings showing energy, character and musical flow. These were baby steps in the Musin school and I would come to understand that one masterclass can only scratch the surface, but it was exciting nonetheless. Yet it was Musin on the podium that made the biggest impression. He was a very small man with an immense presence. With huge, strong and expressive hands he embodied the music, and seemed to be conducting the music from the inside out. There's a temptation for the inexperienced to conduct just the melody. Yet often that is the last thing an orchestra needs. It's the accompaniment that holds it together and brings it to life. This is the motor, and the harmonic foundations on which the melodies have colour, shape and can flow. If this is insecure or lacking character, then the melody will at best be dull and at worst fall apart.

While Musin impressed the West with his inspirational teaching skills, conducting opportunities also opened for him, and he made his Western debut with the Royal Philharmonic Orchestra aged eighty-nine. Talk about taking it slowly! Perhaps this was where I should be looking. I knew a few conductors who had studied in St Petersburg, my friends Gerry Cornelius and Susie Dingle had just returned after a few years of training. They were persuasive. Fifteen years on from Sian's intrepid journey, the East/West divide had ostensibly disappeared, and the whole process was far simpler. It was St Petersburg in Russia, not Leningrad in the Soviet Union, where I was heading. But it was still very alien and required a bit of chutzpah.

Gerry helped me figure out how to get a visa, which included queuing at the Russian Consulate at 7 a.m. in the hope that they'd let you in at 10 a.m., if the queue wasn't too long, and you played your cards right.

ME: How do I play my cards right?

GERRY: Er, I'm not sure. It depends on whether the guy at the gate likes you. Chocolates maybe? Patience? Persistence? It'll all be rather random, and it won't make sense. This is your introduction to Russia!

Early one June morning in 1997, after waiting in line for another few hours, I was handed my visa. I made a quick call to Gerry from a phone box outside the consulate, slowly reading out the words in Cyrillic to check it was legit. I was good to go. I took myself to St Petersburg to take part in a masterclass that was also an audition to be accepted into Musin's class. My first impressions of St Petersburg were of dust, sun 23/7, large buildings with doors made for giants containing a mini-door for humans, and a curious smell of sweat, cheap soap and petrol. This smell is so very distinct-ive, hitting you as you enter Pulkova Airport Arrivals, that on my return trips in the early noughties, as it hit my nos-trils, I would immediately feel happy and excited. I was sad when I returned in 2013 to find the smell has completely disappeared, as better soap and regular changes of clothes are now the norm for most Peterburgians. It wasn't love at first sight for me, and I found it all very intimidating and foreign, but Musin's students (including a few Brits) were warm and friendly. The masterclass was intense, but I seemed to cot-ton on to what he was teaching, and he agreed that I could return in September. With financial help from family, I had enough to allow me to study there for three months.

At the end of those three months, I realised I needed longer. It was a chat one evening after class with my classmate Stuart Stratford (over a couple of glasses of cheap Russian beer) that gave me the push I needed. I returned to the UK, gave up my organist job (and home), and found more funding, which was not easy, since most music-funding bodies don't support conductors. It mostly came from generous members of my family and close friends. Compared with the fees that stu-dents pay these days, it was very cheap, and the cost of living was low. I sold the trumpets that had been languishing on top of the wardrobe for some years, and that funded an intensive course in Teaching English to Speakers of Other Languages. This I rightly surmised would allow me to work part-time. An *Anglichanka* with a teaching qualification could easily pick up work, and about ten to fifteen hours a week was enough to cover food and lodging. Russia was in the throes of a financial crisis in 1998, and the shelves were hardly bulging with food. The rouble was devaluing by the day, which was horrible for many, but I guiltily realised it had advantages for me. I was paid in US dollars, and I kept my savings in my UK account, which stretched further than I had envisaged.

Stuart was finishing his studies and moving back to the UK to become the Conducting Fellow at the Royal Northern College, so I inherited his garret apartment on Liteyny Prospekt. This comprised a kitchen complete with cooker, sink *and* bath (yes, a bath in the kitchen!), cockroaches, and a room with a piano and a large shelf for a mattress, which at a push one might call a mezzanine. There were a few bullet holes in the shared staircase, but my front door was very strong and had three enormous keys, so I felt safe. Over the next two years I moved quite a bit, living in some wonderful places, including the building where Dostoyevsky's Raskolnikov murdered Alyona Ivanovna and Lizaveta, and huge apartments where, living rent-free, I cat sat for expats and Russian artists. One of the cats had to be fed chicken from an expensive 'Western standard' supermarket, so he was eating better than me.

Having said a not too teary farewell to classical languages in 1990, I believed that a rather impressive bookshelf would be all that remained. I had some vague idea that I might follow my grandfather's goal of reading all the Oxford Classical Texts in my retirement – a nice but unrealistic plan. I shall probably never retire anyway. Despite clearly having some affinity with languages and excellent Latin and Greek teachers, I truly believed I was not a linguist. This wasn't helped by our miserable French teacher who loathed teaching English schoolgirls. Rather than rejoicing in our shared linguistic roots, she accused the English of stealing French words. Hardly the most inspiring approach to etymology. In her strong Belgian accent, she would cite historical conflicts between Brits and French with great bitterness: 'You killed Joan d'Arc.' She called me 'Alice au Pays des Merveilles' or 'Merveilles' for short. I'm used to references to my literary namesake, and while I don't find these hilarious, it's usually meant quite affectionately. This title however was delivered with great malice. I'm certainly not the only 'well-educated' Brit to have missed out on the love of communicating in another language, but I wish I'd not sat at the back of French class with my friend Catherine (known as 'Merveilles' friend') working out how we could pass O-level French without doing a stroke of work.

Fortunately, this all changed in my late twenties when I moved to Russia. Yet it was a bumpy learning curve. I was absorbing the Russian language on four different levels: academic, shopping, conducting class and social.

The Cyrillic alphabet is not dissimilar to Greek so that didn't worry me. I knew it only takes a few hours to learn, and then a few weeks to read comfortably. This was essential for geographical bearings in St Petersburg. All the street signs are written in Cyrillic, and I did get lost rather a lot in those first few weeks.

I quickly recognised similarities in Russian grammar – it's like an eccentric version of Ancient Greek. This was going to be interesting. I learned some basics before going to St Petersburg and had one-to-one lessons twice a week at the Conservatoire. We quickly worked through a Russian textbook (*Russian for Everyone*) that used everyday Soviet stories to illustrate grammatical points. Its pedagogical style was not dissimilar to the school Latin and Greek books, and while I probably didn't need to learn all the collective-farm vocabulary, it was nonetheless interesting. My teacher was impressed at how quickly I could grasp complex grammatical structures. I felt safe and comfortable, and probably a little smug.

But then I hit a massive brick wall. I had to speak. Yes, the grammar was similar, but the words were so foreign. It seemed we 'stole' very little from the Slavic group of languages. Even saying 'hello' (*strastvuite*) was a tongue twister. I could, and did, learn the vocabulary, but then I had a great fear of making errors and sounding stupid. Instead of making communication my priority, I focused on speaking correctly. If I couldn't remember the genitive plural ending of such and such a word, then rather than just going for it anyway, I would say nothing or, when possible, resort to English. And while I could read a page of Russian text quite fluently to myself, I panicked when spoken to, and stopped listening, so my aural comprehension wasn't great. I wanted to have a good accent, and not having heard much Russian before, it took some time for my ears to become accustomed to these new sounds, and even longer for the muscles in my mouth and tongue to start making the right movements.

Very slowly and with much hard work I improved. As well as daily private study, I had no choice but to speak in shops, where very few people spoke English. Musin had learned a few phrases (he could say, 'You must go to the point of culmination' surprisingly fluently) but mostly conducting class was in Russian. There were always students who could help and translate initially, and gradually the phrases became more familiar. It was considered the height of bad manners to speak English in front of the Conservatoire orchestra, so that was another vocab-building exercise. The occasional/frequent vodka-influenced social evenings with friends and classmates, and a Russian boyfriend, certainly helped with confidence.

These days my Russian is rusty, as if it's lodged at the very back of my brain, and once I start to use it, slowly it creeps forwards like a shy old friend offering words I forgot I ever knew. It has been useful over the years when working in ballet where, with so many dancers and teachers coming from Russia, it is sometimes the lingua franca. Like many musicians, my accent is very good, which can be misleading.

Rarely taken for an *Anglichanka* and sometimes even taken initially for a Russian, I later confuse people as I struggle to find words and jumble my sentence structure. I'm probably more often taken for an idiot.

The Musin Technique

What was I learning from Musin – or Ilya Alexanzh as he was known by his students and colleagues? What is the St Petersburg school?

When Musin tried to enter Nikolai Malko's conducting class at the Leningrad Conservatoire he was told his baton technique was not good enough. But eventually, after begging Malko, he was given a place. His struggle to achieve this manual dexterity, combined with a passion to conduct, helped shape his future as a teacher. In 1932, when he himself became a professor at the Conservatoire, he also began to analyse and develop a technique. No one previously had formulated such a detailed and clear system of conducting gestures. He gave his last conducting class in the summer of 1999 – nearly seventy years later. He continued to develop this technique and hone his teaching of it throughout those years. His alumni are numerous and include some of the big superstar conductors of our time, including the likes of Valery Gergiev, Yuri Temirikanov, Semyon Bychkov and Teodor Currentzis.

He didn't invent a way of conducting, but through close observation of conductors, he worked out not only how to beat time but how to shape music. Many well-known conductors say that conducting can't really be taught. Musin disagreed. At least he believed and *proved* that a good musician can be taught what to do with their hands to communicate their musical intentions, in the same way that they can be taught a technique for playing an instrument. The Russian penchant and skill for creating artistic systems is something we recognise in Stanislavsky acting teaching, and in the pianists and string players that the country produces. The system is complex and the six-year conducting training that Russian students undergo includes daily work on hands and baton technique.

But as with all Russian artistic systems, Musin's teaching was never technique for technique's sake. Music and musical expression were at the heart of it. Two things that got Musin angry with his students in equal measure were if you just beat time and didn't show the music, or if you were rhythmically unclear, flailing and emoting. The conducting classroom was a highly charged place.

Musin described the main principle of his method thus:

A conductor must make music visible to his musicians
with his hands. There are two components to conducting:
expressiveness and precision. These two components are
dialectically opposed. In fact, they cancel each other out.
A conductor must find a way to bring the two together.

A Beginner's Mini-Guide to the St Petersburg School of Conducting

Precision is essential in making sure the beat is rhythmically clear, so that the orchestra can play together. This could be divided into two basic beats – a click and a circle.

The 'click' is a very precise moment where, as the wrist falls, it hits an imaginary point in the air and rebounds. I prefer to call this a 'bounce' rather than a 'click' as it feels more like hitting a surface and rebounding. It is like the standard beat in all conducting techniques. The placing of these beats, the triangle (in 3) and square (in 4) – the shapes that we learned as children – are slightly different but are easily readable for an orchestra. Some conducting techniques require all clicks to return to the centre of the body, but Musin liked to use a wider area, and he disliked the beat that looks as if it dismisses or wipes away the sound as it goes outwards.

The circle is probably what the St Petersburg school was most famous for. There's no click, but rather the rhythm is controlled by the speed of the hand and arm and the all-important concept of picking up the sound and transferring it from beat to beat. This is excellent for a slow pulse – for example a waltz in 1 that has three beats within it. If executed smoothly and correctly it will give all the precise rhythmic information an orchestra needs but will also allow a smoother (*legato*) sound. The circle can morph into other smooth linking shapes, and the click and circle can blur into each other, providing a large repertoire of beats and phrasal shapes.

The circle was born out of Musin's observation that symphony orchestras, particularly Russian orchestras, play behind the conductor's beat. This is sometimes seen as a bad thing, as if the players don't trust the conductor. Musin realised that the orchestra was simply waiting in that split second for more information and to see what direction the conductor was going before committing to making a sound. The benefit of orchestras playing behind the beat is that the conductor can lead the sound, and control the tempi, but it means that the conductor needs always to maintain contact with the sound and keep moving it along. The danger comes when the conductor waits for the sound; the orchestra will wait even longer, and the music will get slower and slower. I think probably every young conductor has experienced this hell early on in their training and career. A nightmarish slow-motion sense of losing control. (In faster-pulsed music where a precise click is needed, then orchestras need to play exactly on that click.)

How far behind an orchestra plays varies from conductor to conductor, rehearsal to rehearsal, performance to performance, orchestra to orchestra, country to country, and the type of music being played. It is something of a thorny issue. Some conductors hate it, as they feel they have no control. US orchestras play much more on the beat than Europeans, and Russian orchestras play the most behind of them all.

Picking up the sound in your hands is essential in giving a circular beat and can seem counterintuitive to those who meet Musin's technique for the first time. The sound is produced as your hand moves upwards rather than what most of us had been taught – as it touches down onto an imaginary table of sound.

Try this:

Imagine putting your hand into sand, picking up a handful and transferring it to another spot. The sound comes only when you have that sand in your hand and begin moving it to another place (the next beat), and that in turn transfers to the next, and so on – a phrase and line is created. If you're using a baton, then picking up soup with a spoon was a metaphor Musin often used. If you have a grip on that sound, it shouldn't matter how late it comes, you just keep hold and move it on. If you jerk you hand away quickly, you will lose that contact and control.

(Musin learned the word 'jerk' in English and would often say to English-speaking students, 'You jerk!' We knew what he meant and weren't offended.)

When executed properly, the circle has a built-in generosity and confidence – a gathering of the sound, an invitation to play. And it's not just the hand, but the whole arm, from relaxed and strong shoulder, that keeps this contact with the sound.

With this 'picking-up' concept, finding an expressive, characterful beat becomes easier. There are some very complex technical aspects to this school, which take years to master, but there's also a clear practical logic to it. Conducting is a body language and we read body language every day. Therefore, it makes sense that our conducting gestures come out of everyday gestures. For example, the gesture we use when we offer someone a seat can be used to show where the phrase is going to – albeit a stylised and exaggerated version of it.

Anyone who studied with Musin for a decent amount of time will know that his technique will work with pretty much all repertoire. A Musin student should be equipped with such a vast palette of gestures and such a strong sense of connection to the sound that they will be able to draw on this in most situations. There was some criticism or belief in the late 1990s that the Musin technique didn't always work with Western orchestras because the circle was vague and confusing. I think this was more about people misunderstanding it, or not executing it properly. The basic Musin principle gets instantaneous results and immediately makes you look more like an expressive conductor, but a superficial grasp of the system can be dangerous. His fail-safe golden rule was: If your gestures are not working with an orchestra, then change them. In other words, don't stick doggedly to what you believe is good technique, if the orchestra is not responding to it. Try another way of communicating.

That's not to say that his students are the only ones that have this wide palette of gestures. Other teachers and conductors come at this from different directions. Musin had to learn this manual dexterity, as many of us do, but there are some that do it naturally and with very little training. There are also some who successfully rely more on their succinct verbal communication with an orchestra. If I have any criticism of Musin's teaching it was that the focus was sometimes too much on the visual. Sometimes it's knowing exactly what to *say* that makes all the difference.

Musin felt that it was dangerous to talk about great conductors having a hypnotic power over an orchestra. He would say that if we believe great conductors are simply magicians, then we block the way to exploring what truly makes them great. He was pragmatic. He didn't create Valery Gergiev, but he did give him the tools to develop his own style. Those quivering fingers, weaving magic as they do, are founded in a virtuosic technique. A danger when studying conducting is to simply copy other conductors and especially a teacher, but some of that is necessary and good. It takes years for a conductor to find their own style, but with a strong technique like Musin's as a basis, it's possible to develop properly.

There was another reason why Musin was going to work for me. He had no problem teaching women. Russia has an ambiguous relationship with gender equality. In the Communist era women were seen as equal to men in terms of jobs, though it would seem only women were expected to do all the housework and childcare as well. Political correctness is baffling to many Russians, and Musin's view on women conductors was straightforward and robust. He believed that women were just as likely to have the necessary strength and perseverance, but the most important thing for a conductor was to communicate their musical intentions to a group of people. He believed women could do that as well as men, and there was nothing more to discuss. He often had women in his class, and was criticised by some of his colleagues for this.

His class took place three times a week from 3 to 7 p.m. We would take it in turns to conduct two pianists who had been playing for Musin for years and would follow everything we did or failed to do. The classes were open, in that anyone from the conservatoire could observe. Students and professors would often take an opportunity to witness him at work, and there were usually at least twenty people watching and listening. His student numbers fluctuated. Most of them were Russian, and I was aware that the number of Western students wanting Musin's precious time must have impacted on their time, but they were immensely generous and welcoming to us foreigners. Each member of the class would get to conduct at least once a week and we were always learning from each other – waving our hands as we watched. After class we would decamp to a nearby bar and talk about conducting and how the class had gone. We were an odd sight – absentmindedly air-conducting as we talked and drank Baltika beer.

Two mornings a week we were let loose on the conservatoire symphony orchestra. This was a professional ensemble whose full-time job was to play for student conductors. There were other conducting professors (most from the Musin stable) and many more conducting students. It was a huge department. Not surprisingly, this wasn't the most prestigious job a musician could find in the city, and they were a surly and unruly bunch. The principal oboist had a serious smoking habit, which meant he had to leave for a cigarette break every twenty minutes regardless of what was being played. I suspect one or two of them might have had a few strong drinks to help start the day. They didn't make a great sound, but they did follow the conductors. Every couple of months, Musin would explode at them, and they would behave for a while. Sian still has a splinter from an antique chair that shattered into pieces when Musin threw it, not quite at a trumpeter, but certainly in his direction.

I wasn't studying for a formal degree, but as well as conducting, other classes were available at a very reasonable fee. In addition to Russian lessons, I elected to study aural training, and also string technique. Honing your ear is always good, and never having played a stringed instrument, I had much to learn. Conductors need to know how to talk to string players about the sound they want, so some theoretical grasp of technique is important.

With all Musin's complex technical emphasis, there was never a moment when music wasn't at the heart of his teaching and this heart was big, fierce and generous. He had lived through the whole of Communism, during the Second World War he miraculously escaped the Germans and was evacuated to Tashkent, and he'd experienced cruel anti-Semitism that cut short his conducting career. Yet it was music and his students that kept him alive and positive. What struck me most on arriving in St Petersburg less than ten years after the end of the Cold War was the importance of the arts and music over materialism. There were the *Novy Russki* (New Russians) with their flashy cars, but they were a minority and not in my social circle. There's no doubting the downsides of Communism, but as a society Russians certainly valued the arts, albeit quite a conservative version. Musin had seen it all, and nothing fazed him. Music mattered more than anything – except his family and his students. He would make jokes about the lack of food on the shelves during the financial crisis, but only because it allowed him to describe the concept of picking up the sound: 'You used to be able to pick up food from the shelves and put it in your bag, just as you pick up sound and move it to the next beat, but now there's nothing there, as if there's no sound.'

Music affected him so deeply that as his conducting career reignited, he often chose the kitschest of kitsch music (Tchaikovsky's *Capriccio Italien,* Rimsky-Korsakov's *Capriccio Espagnol*) rather than serious Shostakovich symphonies. He was a year older than Shostakovich, they were classmates, and he knew his music intimately. But the angst in Shostakovich's music that today is still so appealing to the angry young well-fed musician was too much like the real life he had lived. He chose music that made him feel happy. I loved that. His repertoire choice also had to do with stamina. Short light pieces are physically less demanding. His eyesight was poor towards the end, so everything had to be from memory.

I never forget a class when one student was conducting the finale to Tchaikovsky's Sixth (and last) Symphony – the *Pathétique* – a great honour to be allowed to bring that to Ilya Alexanj. The finale is about dying. No matter how heartfelt his interpretation, and how hard this student tried, it was never going to impress this nonagenarian with a serious heart and lung condition. Musin stood up to demonstrate, and as he conducted the final bars (the cellos and double-basses: a heartbeat slowly fading to nothing), the atmosphere in the room became dark and worrying. There was always a fear one of us would tip his heart over the edge, and usually it was when he got angry – raised voices and colourful language. Yet that anger seemed to feed his energy, and this was more dangerous. The music was life-sapping. It was a brilliant lesson, but as the student walked back to his seat, Musin sent out a plea to the class: 'Something more cheerful next please!' Luckily someone had bought the *Nutcracker Suite*. Within seconds, Musin was up on his feet, looking thirty years younger, his blue eyes full of spark and cheekiness.

SIAN EDWARDS: Musin always wanted nothing less than a performance from his students, even just with the two pianos. He expected us to conduct from memory. Sometimes he'd stop you mid-flow and sort something that needed correcting, but other times he let you do the whole movement or large sections of it. He had an engagement with his students, and a continual offering of suggestions. Everything he did was connected naturally to something musical. I was immediately drawn to Musin's honesty and gentle directness, which made me feel safe.

On 6 June 1999, rather fittingly Pushkin's 200th birthday, Musin died, aged ninety-five, just a few days after he had been teaching us. We all knew this day would come quite soon, but it was sad, nonetheless. I'd only ever been to English funerals where, even at my father's, there was something of a party atmosphere. Not so in Russia, and it was refreshingly cathartic. As we gazed at the open coffin, the Mariinsky orchestra, conducted by some of his most famous former students, played excerpts of suitably mournful music, ending with Gergiev conducting that very same Tchaikovsky *Pathétique* finale. We decamped in buses for the burial, after which small plastic glasses of vodka were handed round, and then we returned to the Mariinsky for a banquet. Toasts were given, and then the students went back to Musin's apartment, where there were more toasts, and we watched videos of him conducting. The next day we all met again in his apartment and now we could tell fun stories about him, and of course drink more toasts. We met again the following week to pay our respects at the graveside, and back to his apartment – and more toasts. An awful lot of vodka – ironic since Musin was a teetotaller, but it was a proper farewell.

During these two years I had many lessons with Leonid Korchmar, a conductor at the Mariinsky and Musin's assistant. Musin was sometimes ill or away on tour. The year he died he conducted twice in Japan and Tel Aviv. It made sense for me to stay one more year with Korchmar because I knew I still had a way to go. Thanks to an expat business community, and the British Council, I was able to put on concerts with some orchestras in the city – more repertoire, more podium time. A conductor was gradually taking shape.

The Conducting Teacher

As with all musicians, many conductors include some teaching in their portfolio of work. Some work almost full-time teaching while others give occasional masterclasses. There are as many different styles of teaching as there are conductors, but good conductors often make good teachers. Communication is at the heart of both, and conductors that don't see themselves as teachers are often quite surprised at how much knowledge they have to impart, when they are given the opportunity to teach.

I started teaching in 2013 when I founded the Women Conductors programme, and it has remained part of my working life ever since. I have no doubt that it has made me a better conductor. It's like holding up a mirror to yourself, seeing the mistakes you might make, but at a distance. When I teach, I draw on a mixture of what I was taught and what I wish someone had told me. It's not so difficult for a Musin student to teach, simply because we were taught so well ourselves, and the handing down of the St Petersburg school continues, and not solely in Russia. That's why I particularly like teaching with Sian Edwards. We speak the same language, and I always learn from her. Of course, we give our own take on it, but the core principles are strong.

In recent years the time I spend teaching has increased, helped by the possibilities of Zoom. For one-to-one teaching it's perfectly workable, and now I have regular students all over the world.

I was in the middle of running a conducting programme at the National Concert Hall in Dublin in March 2020 at the start of the Covid pandemic and over the next few months I started making short videos of exercises – 'the scales and arpeggios' of conducting if you like. Clearly no one could practise in front of an orchestra for a while, but a great deal of work can be done in the privacy of your own room, and not just poring over scores. All you need is a room big enough to swing a baton. I adapted the exercises I was given when I first went to Russia, always trying to be loyal to Musin's ethos that technique and musical expression shouldn't be separated. But this is just the building blocks. I don't want my students just to copy me.

MARIN ALSOP: Starting a career conducting is very hard. There are a hundred musicians and only one conductor, so opportunities are hard to come by. I tell my students, 'You have to practise this instrument even if it's air-practising' – like air-guitar. You must figure out what you are going to do, because when you stand in front of a hundred people, it's not going to magically work. But that's the interesting thing about conducting. Imagining that you can do

121

something without ever really doing it because you make no sound. It's the daydreaming part.

I hope that all my students, besides being clear, should look completely different. I'm not wanting to create an army of mini-Marins. A conductor is trying to bring out the essence of music, and that's why teaching is so fascinating. It's about building the best possible artist from the raw material that they bring to the table.

Another busy conductor who somehow found time to teach as well was Bramwell Tovey. His breadth of experience and generosity combined to make him a wonderful mentor and teacher. When he was young, conducting teaching was nowhere near as sophisticated, but there were paid positions for young conductors. Bramwell started conducting the London Festival Ballet at the age of twenty-two:

I think I learned everything my conducting teacher at the Royal Academy could tell me in three weeks. It was conducting experience and trial and error that helped me develop.

A natural and thoughtful communicator like Bramwell is naturally going to be a fine teacher. These days a kinder form of teaching is expected, and this is a good thing.

SIAN EDWARDS: There was this long tradition around the world, that if anyone put their head above the parapet to be a conductor, the first thing that would happen is that they would get pretty brutally knocked down. The ones that could get up from the floor were deemed to be the toughest and could therefore survive the profession.

There might be some young conductors who need a serious reality check, but I don't believe that this form of bullying achieves that. More often it just discourages the sensitive musician, who does have something to communicate. I'm glad to say that tradition is dying out, but that's not to say that teachers aren't demanding and tough. Rather than the one-to-one tuition of instrumental teaching, on most conducting courses class is the focus, and students are expected to conduct two pianos in front of their peers. Because Sian is a sought-after teacher, there are usually a few guests watching too. She expects the students to come with something, to perform, to be put on the spot, and this is important for the student conductor's development.

Masterclasses

A good way of furthering one's career is to take part in masterclasses around the world, but I decided that wasn't for me. They were fiendishly expensive, and I needed to earn money and start paying off my student loans. I knew I had so much to learn, but I was thirty by the time I left Russia, and I felt it was time to put my official student days behind me. I wanted to learn on the job. I had been taking part in masterclass-style lessons several times a week for three years in St Petersburg. I didn't feel the need to fly halfway round the world at great expense for an hour of podium time with a famous name, just so I could add it to my C.V. I didn't want anyone messing with a technique I knew was excellent. What I needed was rehearsal technique and podium experience. This could be found by getting work and being part of a professional environment.

I have always struggled with one big aspect of the masterclass. The person giving the masterclass is in charge, thereby undermining the person standing on the podium. With the many gifted conducting teachers, there is a sensitivity to this, and it can be an excellent learning environment. Sad to say, there are some maestros that see this as an opportunity to make themselves look good by bullying and humiliating the young conductor on the podium. One could argue that this is exactly what the bumptious ones who frankly should be taken down a peg or two need, but for the more sensitive it can be soul-destroying. In St Petersburg I decided to be a sponge and take everything I could from my teachers. Musin and Korchmar were tough but also kind. I didn't intend to continue working in Russia; it didn't matter if I looked a complete idiot and had no authority on the podium. I knew I was learning and could apply it all somewhere new later, when I was in charge.

It might well be that I was missing out by not taking masterclasses from other teachers around the world.

TIANYI LU: I have learned so much from all the masterclasses I have taken part in. Even when the people giving them have been difficult to get along with, as soon as I figured out that all that extra stuff was about them and not me, I just focused on what I could get out of it. Even when I don't agree with them, there's always something to be learned. You can discard what doesn't work for you later on. I had interesting conversations with fellow participants too.

Bramwell Tovey maintained the collective noun for conductors is a 'carvery'. They can be a fascinating group of people to talk to, and I had spent years with some wonderful Musin classmates. As we moved into a new millennium, I was looking forward to meeting musicians outside the 'carvery' and gaining new perspectives.

6: Careers

The Label

When do you start calling yourself a conductor? When you have conducted one or two concerts at school, or when you start studying conducting full-time? When do you start calling yourself a professional conductor? When do people start calling you 'maestro'? (Not so much in the UK, but in many countries that's still how they address us, which personally I find deeply embarrassing or just hilarious.) When you have a degree – a qualification telling the world that you are a conductor – or the first time you get paid for a job with an amateur or professional orchestra, or when you're working full-time, and most of your earnings come from conducting? It could be any of these and anything in between. There are no rules, though I can admit to raising an eyebrow at some young people who will announce they are a conductor after one or two lessons and the odd concert with a group of friends. For years I felt it safer to say, 'I hope to become a conductor.'

In Russia where we students ate, drank and slept conducting, it was a more comfortable label to own.

SIAN EDWARDS: It was a gradual and natural progression for me. Not until my second year in Russia, when I was standing in front of the mirror practising, do I remember thinking, 'Perhaps now I can begin to think of myself as a conductor.'

Most Russian conducting students had been told very young (mid- to late teens) that this was to be their well-trodden path, and a more regulated form of training and competition allowed them to feel comfortable with this. It was assigned to them rather than a self-appointed title.

Not so much in the West, and especially not in the last century.

ANTONIO PAPPANO: I had absolutely no ambition to be a conductor when I was young. I just got to know singers and the vocal repertoire which became so important to me later.

BARRY WORDSWORTH: At school and music college it was always more a case of: 'Well, one day you might conduct, but you'd better learn to be a good musician first.'

The industry has changed a great deal over the past decades, and although there has always been a fascination with the *wunderkind* brilliant conductor who sweeps to fame in their early twenties (Leonard Bernstein and Simon Rattle for example), the obsession with youth has become more fashionable in recent years. It is probably a cyclical thing and doesn't preclude older conductors from continuing to work. Having spent so many years growing into this profession, valuing not only the musical knowledge I've gained, but also reaching a modicum of maturity and wisdom, it's only in the past decade that I've begun to feel I can do my job well. Like most older conductors and orchestral players, I have a natural mistrust for this attraction to the new and shiny, and worry that experience might not be valued enough.

It is good to dig a bit deeper and find out what's really going on beyond the plethora of social-media announcements of young conductors about to make it big. There's no doubt that the desire to become a conductor is on the increase, and that the quality of conducting pedagogy around the world is at its highest. There are many more opportunities, including some supportive and interesting competitions out there, and these can help young conductors develop and not be left to crash and burn when the novelty of the bright young thing has worn off.

Competitions

I took part in a couple of competitions and got through the early rounds reasonably well. The first was a small workshop-style competition of young UK and Irish conductors, and with Martyn Brabbins (another former Musin student) in charge, it turned out to be an excellent learning environment. It was a conversation with him shortly after that helped me decide to go to Russia. The other was not so enjoyable and not helped by a bullying panel member (revered in the conducting world) who made childish and very audible noises at the back of the orchestra whenever a candidate, including me, didn't conduct to his taste. It was initially stressful and frightening, then actually quite irritating. I quickly decided this wasn't for me and that I'd be better focusing my energies in other ways. Sian Edwards has been on the panel for many conducting competitions in recent years, and it's heartening to hear how things have changed for the better.

SIAN EDWARDS: There seem to be more competitions than ever, or at least some have been resurrected and have a higher profile now because they are streamed. It's good that everyone can see what the judges are seeing, which makes it a much more open debate about the choices of who goes through. Every competition is different in terms of what they are looking for, what stage the conductors are entering the profession, and how much support they will need to develop.

It seems that orchestras have woken up to the fact that they need to nurture conductors, but competitions are not for everyone.

SIAN EDWARDS: When students ask me whether they should apply for a competition, I ask if they really have time to learn the repertoire. If they get knocked out in the first round, it won't matter too much if they have really invested time in learning the repertoire. They should understand that it's the music that matters most, and they can walk away knowing some wonderful scores. Competitions are an opportunity to be seen and heard, but I always stress that they are only for people who feel they can go into combat as it were, and it is just one way of getting there.

In the best competitions, conductors must show not just what they do with their hands, but how they rehearse, and this is what sorts the sheep from the goats.

SIAN EDWARDS: As jury members we are trying to see beyond our own personal taste to how these conductors relate to the sound: do they want something, are they imaginative and interesting? That's the most important thing. In the video stage we are going to miss people who don't have good hands, but who might be fantastic musicians. To them I would say, 'Don't go into competitions, find another route.' They can become just as successful.

I am ambivalent about competitions, but I do believe they offer one way of regulating this almost unregulatable pro-fession, at least in the early stages, and for a certain group of conductors. Most assistant conductor positions involve some form of competition, and a well-known professional orchestra will get hundreds of applicants. Young conductors are prepared to up sticks and move anywhere for these op-portunities. Recently, an orchestra who didn't put a regional limit on their application criteria (i.e. requiring residency in the country or region of the world) had over seven hundred applicants.

In summer 2020, some orchestras were still able to hold their competitions, and the live-streaming of these events became more popular than ever. Tianyi was on a roll and won two competitions in the space of a few weeks: the Guido Cantelli Conducting Competition in Italy, and the Sir Georg Solti International Conductors' Competition in Germany.

TIANYI LU: My priority in preparing for these competitions was creativity. I analysed the scores, worked out patterns, phrase lengths, and told stories. I found the energy of the pieces in my body by dancing. I did a lot of meditation and yoga to be rooted so that in the moment, despite the fear, I could access my childlike, non-judgemental side. I asked myself, 'How am I going to inspire an orchestra in just twenty minutes?' Over the years I had been discouraged from using metaphorical language when rehearsing, something I do instinctively, but I noticed that the people in competitions who got noticed were the ones who did just that. I went back to being true to my own ideas and backed it up with straighter technical language too.

Competitions work well for young conductors ready and suited to the fast-track process. Although the age limit is usually thirty or thirty-five, it seems to be conductors between twenty-five and thirty who thrive best in this environment. From the cohort of young conductors interviewed (Olivia Clarke, Tianyi Lu, Jonathon Heyward, Ben Glassberg and Kalena Bovell) they have all been winners, whether in official competitions, or a highly competitive audition process for an assistantship position. This is not for the faint hearted.

KALENA BOVELL: Before my audition for the assistantship job at Memphis Symphony Orchestra, I sat in my hotel room and asked myself why I was nervous. When I realised that my fears were unfounded because I had done so much preparation, I talked myself into a calmer state of mind. Then I stood in front of the orchestra, and it all came right back. My baton was shaking, and something happened, I hit the stand and my music fell off. So, I said to the orchestra, 'Let's do that again, and I'll try not to hurt myself this time.' The orchestra laughed and it became a very human moment. I realised I was just making music with a wonderful group of people.

Once they have that job, then their trial is by no means over. Regularly conducting a professional orchestra, probably for the first time out of music college, can and should be a tough and steep learning curve. Feedback from orchestral players can be invaluable, but it needs to be well managed, if it's not to turn into bullying. Many instrumentalists work in education; perhaps they coach and teach their instrument in a conservatoire as well as playing in an orchestra. They care about how they communicate with young conductors, and this help is golden. But it can't be assumed that every member of the orchestra has that skill – naturally or otherwise. After all, they have been hired for their skill on an instrument and their ability to play at the highest level in an ensemble, and not as an educator.

Conductors need to be able to take criticism, especially early in their careers, but that criticism should come from a place of mutual respect and trust. It is a professional and not a student environment, so the experienced player needs to feel that the person on the podium will lead and allow them to do their job properly. They also need to understand that this person is still learning to do their job. That is a big ask and can make for a very uncomfortable and frustrating relationship on both sides.

The days of the dictatorial conductor are largely gone, in most orchestras, but the legacy of the bullying conductor remains. There is still a residue, a collective memory in professional orchestras all over the world of being bullied as a group, and sometimes that will manifest itself in players in turn bullying the weakest among them. A young conductor can be ripe for picking, and even well-established conductors can come under fire, especially with a new orchestra. A bullied conductor will either give up or toughen up, and with wisdom and self-awareness they could well thrive in the industry, but I don't believe bullying should be a necessary or helpful rite of passage. Developing a thick skin is important, but if that skin becomes so thick that the conductor stops listening and empathising with their musicians, then that is surely a bad thing. In this environment, conductors are more likely to become defensive, which will often manifest itself in aggressive behaviour. Pomposity is another option for the un-self-aware and insecure, and it can be truly grating for an experienced orchestral player to have to deal with this, especially in a young conductor. Performing music requires a whole gamut of emotions and sensitivities, and a conductor who can't tap into those is going to fall short.

As part of the Royal Philharmonic Society Women Conductors programme, we have teamed up with the Royal Northern Sinfonia in a two-year project. We not only give talented upcoming female conductors some podium time, but also explore that relationship between a trained but relatively inexperienced conductor and a professional orchestra. We are looking at ways of developing a meaningful conversation between orchestral players and conductors, including giving constructive feedback. We are able to create an excellent atmosphere and a safe space to experiment with these ideas. We are not providing a solution, but there is great willingness to explore this conundrum.

Different Paths

The wonderful thing about this profession is that there are plenty of routes for the hard-working, talented, dedicated and determined. Not all assistant positions are official, and that was especially true when I started out. Post-Russia, a mixture of assistantships, three years in a full-time position at a large Swedish opera house, my own smaller-scale engagements, long tours and performance runs with plenty of podium time: these experiences allowed me to develop and keep learning. It took a long time, with many disappointments and frustrations, but I was never out of work and a fully formed conductor gradually emerged.

One path for a young conductor is to attach yourself to an established conductor and become a useful pair of ears in the auditorium, showing how well you know the music. That conductor might hand you the baton sometimes, and the orchestra, including the management, could start finding you useful too. Doors can open. This unofficial form of climbing the career ladder is as old as the hills and showing that initiative is no bad thing. I would say, however, that this style of networking is better suited to the male conductor. Well over 90 per cent of established conductors are male. A certain amount of charm and flattery is necessary to get noticed by them, and it's no surprise that offering to buy a male conductor a drink after a performance or hanging around their dressing room is an option that women might shy away from. That is the reason why, when I am asked to find an assistant, and if no competition or audition is involved in the appointment, I will actively look for a woman first. This seems a fair way of tipping the balance slightly.

Finding the right path and making sure you are well equipped is no easy challenge, particularly if you come to conducting later. Today, with such high-quality teaching, a good baton technique is a given, and if you're a young conductor, that is expected. For conductors transitioning from another discipline within music, particularly if they are well established in that area, then an orchestra might accept a certain lack of technique because they bring so much musical experience and expertise with them. The orchestra can fill in the gaps if necessary. There have been and always will be conductors falling into that category and many will do well.

A Marketeer

Once the initial competition/audition stage of a young conductor's career is over, then they are unlikely ever to apply for a job again. Jobs are rarely advertised, and work is nearly all got by word of mouth and reputation. Having a website and a social-media profile is important for most unless they are incredibly well known and have a very active and influential agent. Finding a good agent who is prepared to take on a conductor isn't easy. Reputations can grow (or fade) naturally, and one job will often lead to another. The music world is small, and people talk. Not only doing a job well but also being a good colleague is important, and this can be confusing for those who still think the dictator conductor is acceptable. Some conductors, perhaps with mentors who help steer them and say good things about them to others, will find their career path to be smooth. Others have a rockier time of it, and it takes longer. Perhaps they had some breaks earlier on and weren't ready or were unable to capitalise on them. Some have a feast-and-famine experience. Outside influences such as a financial or political crisis can impact directly on conductors as well.

Conductors must sell themselves and network. The inherently modest conductor will have a reticence to do this and might even think it a bit vulgar. They might get lucky anyway, but it's unlikely. Hoping your talents will be spotted without making any effort to show them to people is naive. I find it useful to be business-like about this and see my conducting as my wares. If I were making beautiful teapots and needed to sell them, I wouldn't hide them in a cupboard and expect everyone to know how beautiful they were. I think the younger generation of conductors, used to social media, are more comfortable with this.

If a singer or instrumentalist wants to be heard, they can sing or play to someone in an audition. Auditions are quite hard to get, and the industry also relies on word of mouth for hiring, but it is even harder for a conductor to demonstrate their abilities. They can send video footage, and this has become much easier. A YouTube link rather than a DVD (or back in the day a large VHS cassette) is not only easier and cheaper to send to multiple people; it is much easier for the recipient to take a quick look, even if it's just on their phone. The problem is that getting good video footage is incredibly expensive. Union rules on recording rights for orchestral players (in the UK certainly) are rightly stringent but this means that getting permission for a conductor to make a video with a professional orchestra is very hard. Conductors rely more on inviting promoters, and if their performance is outside a large city, the number of people who might consider coming is very small indeed. In any case, since the rehearsal process is where a conductor really shows their mettle, a concert won't give the whole picture.

A conductor doesn't need to be aggressive about networking – in fact that can be detrimental – but sometimes they need to persuade people they can do the job, simply by describing what they do rather than actually doing it. Those two skills don't always come together. The industry relies, in part, on engaging people who look and sound like a conductor. This plays well for the white male, though it has dramatically improved in recent years.

Paul Jacobs is a partner at Grant Thornton Ireland, sponsors of the Female Conductor Programme at the National Concert Hall in Dublin. Not simply financing this programme, the company has also involved itself in running workshops in leadership and communication skills, which has been fascinating and invaluable to the participants.

PAUL JACOBS: Navigating a conducting career seems to be one of the hardest businesses I have ever encountered. Conductors must identify and secure opportunities that are not always visible or obvious, which makes it particularly difficult to establish one's reputation and career.

Starting your own orchestra is a good way of getting things moving. This is easily achievable if you're rich, and some very successful conductors throughout history have done just that. But there are other ways, such as finding sponsors, and other interested parties, and having a good head for business can be so useful.

It is perfectly possible to enjoy a successful career in conducting and never hold an official position with an orchestra. Most orchestras and opera companies engage guest conductors for a certain number of performances in a season. Repeat invitations for the ones they like is the norm. There is an element of insecurity in this, as with any freelance career, but there are great advantages too. There's so much variety, travel around the world, and opportunities to work with so many different artists. It keeps life fresh and exciting.

Language and Culture

The importance of concise verbal communication and the international nature of the classical music industry means most conductors have good linguistic skills. Native English speakers can get away with speaking only one language, but most make that extra effort, and in opera it's essential to have a decent grasp of Italian at least, and probably German and French too. This is another pleasurable and challenging part of the job for me.

At the turn of the millennium, with Russian under my belt, and a career in opera conducting beckoning, Italian was the next to be tackled, along with German. The former was not so hard with a background in Latin, and even German grammar didn't present so many problems. My skill in both languages is based around opera libretto vocabulary, which makes for limited conversations, including embarrassing an Italian waiter when I ordered what I thought was a snack.

Swedish has ended up being my third language. I was a chorus master and assistant conductor at Gothenburg for three years after I left Russia, and initially resisted learning Swedish, since it wasn't one of the operatic languages and I didn't think I'd be staying very long. I also couldn't get the *Muppets* Swedish Chef out of my head and felt a bit silly speaking it. The only people I met who didn't speak almost perfect English were Eastern Europeans who spoke Russian, so we could communicate. Eventually I put some effort in because I was beginning to feel like an arrogant British expat who doesn't bother speaking the language in the country where they have been welcomed. I moved back to the UK in 2004 but returned to Sweden to work quite regularly from 2015. In 2018 I decided to stretch myself and took a B2 Level examination, thanks to which, according to the snappily named Common European Framework of Reference for Languages, I can 'achieve most goals and express myself on a range of topics'.

Swedish is not a terribly difficult language for English-speakers. We 'stole' a lot of words from the Vikings; the Swedes have also stolen French and German words, and the grammar is closer to English than any other language I know. The pronunciation is a challenge, but the main obstacle, even with all that study, is that I rarely meet someone whose English is worse than my Swedish. I rely on patient friends and colleagues to practise, and in the fast pace of a rehearsal you don't want to be using your colleagues as unpaid teachers. I have only ever spoken Swedish with Swedes, so my accent is decent though for some reason I'm told I sound Finnish with a trace of Russian – more exotic than a vicar's daughter from Norfolk at least! Yet still the performance anxiety kicks in sometimes, and the fear of linguistic errors can paralyse me. The danger and stupidity of this hit home recently during a lovely candlelit evening with Swedish friends. I was watching Paulina leaning back as her long blonde curly hair got dangerously close to a naked flame and wondering how best to say 'Be careful, you're about to set light to your hair!' I found just the right phrase very slowly, and in the nick of time. '*Vad fan* (WTF), Alice! you could have just said it in English!'

For rehearsal purposes the lack of sophisticated vocabulary can be useful, as I become more direct, which is not a bad thing. And relying on physical communication is always good. In 2013 I was invited to conduct Britten's opera *The Rape of Lucretia* at the Mariinsky Theatre. It was a thrilling experience with the performers putting that extra Russian *dusha* (soul) into the score, and I worked very hard with the singers on the English text and style. They seemed to understand me most of the time, and if I struggled to find the right word, then I could resort to English for clarification.

Conductors who are brought up bilingual have a huge advantage, and particularly for opera. Because so many work and travel around the world, it's not unusual for them to be multilingual. It's harder for native English speakers where the necessity is less, but it's useful to know a few useful words and phrases in a variety of languages.

JANE GLOVER: When I'm conducting in Germany, I always start the rehearsal in German even if I later find I resort to English. That way, they know I understand German and will be less likely to talk about me within my earshot.

No conductor wants to hear what an orchestra really thinks of them. Constructive feedback is one thing, but grumbles are usually unhelpful. I did the same thing when I conducted the Royal Danish Ballet. I can't speak Danish but it's sufficiently like Swedish for me to get a good gist, so I spoke a little Swedish at the start just as a warning. In many countries, particularly Scandinavia, the standard of English is so good that even references to British TV comedies will get a laugh, but it's dangerous to assume everyone will understand. The competitive and beautifully international nature of our industry means that it's very rare to find an ensemble in any country made up entirely of musicians born there. Finding concise, simple yet unpatronising vocabulary is an art.

Whatever country I am in, I try at the very least to learn a few choice phrases. Marin Alsop has regular Zoom meetings with her Taki Alsop Conducting Fellows – an international team of upcoming female conductors from all over the world.

> MARIN ALSOP: We put together a list of phrases that conductors use in rehearsals, then each conductor translated, and transliterated it into their own language.

This is a wonderful idea, and I would love to see conductors around the world sharing and expanding this resource. It is important to pick up something of the culture of a new country, and language can help with this. While Western classical music around the world shares a common language, with similar orchestral layouts, and rehearsal schedules, there are subtle differences that can catch out the foreign conductor.

> MARIN ALSOP: I think it would be useful for young conductors to have a kind of cultural immersion course, so they don't unwittingly cause offence.

When working with an orchestra in Eastern Europe, I had a disastrous first few days of rehearsal and then tried losing my temper and shouted at them – just once. It seemed they were waiting for me to show I was strong enough, and from that moment on they were fine. It was an initiation that I had missed because that kind of shouting would be unacceptable back home.

ANTONIO PAPPANO: In Italy what helps me is my English/
American background. Italians always go in search of
the lyricism in music and that's wonderful. But Italy is a
culture of the individual and an orchestra by its very nature
is not that. I've been fighting with my heart and soul not
to be the cruel beast they expect of a conductor, but I do
have explosions of anger that come out when it's just a
case of quietening them down so we can work. That would
never happen in London.

The multi-lingual Tony would have no problem expressing
his anger in Italian, English, German or French, but for most
of us it is very dangerous and could have quite unintended
results. The story of the anonymous conductor who lost his
temper with a British orchestra some decades ago has gone
down in history when he shouted: 'You think I know fuck
nothing, but I tell you I know fuck all!'

A Title

Many conductors enjoy rewarding and fully satisfying careers
without ever holding a permanent titled position, taking up
regular guest engagements with different orchestras, often
being invited back multiple times. But most orchestras and
opera and ballet companies do have fixed conducting positions, and depending on the size they can include a music
director/artistic director, principal conductor and principal
guest conductor. These come with a two-year, five-year or

permanent contract and the security of that alone is very attractive. This position puts a label round the conductor's neck that says, 'This person is worth hiring.' In most cases, at least in the UK, these positions are not advertised.

Music director posts are not normally full-time, but if they are, there is always some allowance for the conductor to take outside engagements. To some degree they can choose the repertoire they want to do, giving them the opportunity to experiment in a structured way. They have their hands on the budget, and with that comes responsibility. The canny music director is attentive to how they build the orchestra's reputation in the context of their own career. Their position also gives them some power because usually they have some influence on who else the orchestra will invite to conduct.

A principal conductor might have less control and do fewer performances; a principal guest conductor less again. But that's not to say these positions aren't attractive and prestigious. Because they take up less time in the year, it's possible to hold a few at the same time, and they also require less administrative work.

An Office Job

As with nearly all professions today, a certain amount of sitting behind the computer is a given for a conductor. Even with the help of managers and agents, a complicated portfolio career will require excellent organisational skills. For concerts, and larger-scale productions such as operas, conductors are normally consulted on rehearsal schedules, casting singers and soloists, the size and seating of the orchestra, and editions that are to be used. Sometimes these meetings are squeezed in between rehearsals and performances, and it's very common that the compulsory fifteen-minute break for the orchestra in a three-hour rehearsal will be taken up with people asking 'quick questions' of the conductor. I never sit down for a three-hour orchestral rehearsal, and while I'm on the podium I don't notice this, but sometimes I've found simply getting to a chair in the break is quite a challenge as I run the gauntlet of people trying to do their job and needing an answer from me on all sorts of things.

For a music director these pressures are multiplied many times over, and the size of this job will partly depend on the ambitions of the conductor for their ensemble. Their desire to be creative and do justice to the position will create more work, and sometimes this can suck them dry. There are uncreative aspects to this too, like looking at budgets, attending fundraising events and talking to donors. It can certainly be a challenge to one's personal life, particularly if the music director doesn't live in the city where they hold the position. But there are many upsides to the position.

BARRY WORDSWORTH: Sir Colin Davis used to say that part of the responsibility of the music director is to be the conscience of his orchestra, to be a guardian of the profession. If you're with an orchestra and the same management team for a long period, you can build up a feeling, not just about crotchets and quavers and whether someone is playing sharp or flat, but also work out what the orchestra is like and how it fits into the musical life of the community. It's wonderful but you can't do it if you're there for just a few weeks of the year.

If you have a supportive management team around you, then you shouldn't need to do the basic admin, but I think it is important to get involved, and make sure the music director has a voice in decision-making. Creating an orchestra with a sound that you want is important, but if that is already good, then you must make sure that it doesn't get eroded during your tenure.

It is not at all surprising to me that of the older generation of conductors I interviewed for this book, except for Marin Alsop, it is the men whose careers run in a steady trajectory that naturally leads to them holding the most prestigious positions in the industry. With a cursory look at the winners and runners-up in international competitions, I look forward to a more inclusive future, where musical leaders are better represented by wider society.

It is a tough profession and the unregulated nature of it is sometimes unfair, but I'm not sure a regulated version would be any better. If every job was an audition, then only those who audition well would get work, and some take longer to impress. As a natural optimist, what I love about this insecure profession is that it's never boring and there's always hope.

Part II

7: Opera

Bafflement

The first opera I experienced live was Verdi's *La traviata* at Glyndebourne when I was sixteen. I wish I could say it lit the flames for a lifelong love of opera, but sadly not. A schoolfriend's parents generously paid for my ticket and plied us with wine at the long interval, so I have almost no memory of the second half. In any case I was deeply confused five minutes into Act I scene i. This most complex and thrilling of art forms does require some pre-performance homework. At the very least reading an intelligible synopsis (there are some badly written and confusing ones out there) and listening to a few highlights will certainly help. I was told it was about a courtesan, and since I didn't know what that word meant, I was none the wiser, and my already decent classical language education would help not one iota with sung Italian. Yes, it was exciting when the chorus and orchestra were in full swing, but because I couldn't follow the plot, the opera's dramatic potency was utterly lost on me. It looked rather impressive: sets with huge doors stretching up to the fly of the stage – you expected giants not humans to walk through them. The voices sounded superhuman too, and not having heard this music live before, it seemed a bit overblown. It was so far removed from choral music and what I thought was singing. Even with my privileged education, the language of opera had me utterly baffled.

Thirty-five years later, making my first visit to Canada in February 2020, I was in operatic heaven conducting one of the greatest works in the Italian bel canto repertoire – *Norma*. The 'Casta Diva' aria is what makes this work so famous, and sublime it may be, for but me it is the heart-breaking dramatic power of the final scene – the terrible sacrifice, the agonising pain of parental love and forgiveness – that does it. I no longer hear opera as overblown; rather this is an intimate, visceral language I understand.

It is the camaraderie of the working environment that I love too. As soon as the audience burst into applause at the end of the opera, I mouthed a big 'thank you' to the orchestra, shook hands with the leader and front-desk players, and quickly began my journey to the stage for the bows. To reach the stage from the pit in Calgary's Jubilee Hall, as in most large theatres, involves quite an undignified dash through doors, down corridors and up winding staircases. A member of stage management was waiting outside the pit to guide me, and there was no time to dawdle. In my preoccupied state, and much to the amusement of the orchestra, I managed to walk into a cupboard at the back of the pit. At subsequent performances the percussionist kindly held the exit door open for me, enthusiastically waving at me, just in case.

Singing

Growing up, our house was full of singing. My mother, at the piano, had a true gift for teaching songs and allowing children to sing tunefully, naturally and unpretentiously. Our family car, a retired and temperamental London black cab, didn't have a radio, and we always sang – raucously – as my sister and I danced around unseatbelted, with the dog in the spacious back, our parents closing the glass partition when we got too loud. We greeted my father's medieval lute songs with limited enthusiasm, but he also had a decent repertoire in Norfolk sea shanties and some very tuneful spiritual songs. He wasn't a 'happy clappy' Christian, and as a former member of Coventry Cathedral Choir he was steeped in that rich Anglican church music tradition. Yet he was also drawn to folk, sacred music he could accompany on a guitar, and especially informal music that might attract young families into coming to church. My sister and I did watch *Top of the Pops*, but also (I'm slightly embarrassed to admit) *Songs of Praise*. I rarely go to church these days, but I still love the strong melody of an Anglican hymn.

We (my sister and I, *not* my parents) loved musicals and knew every single word of *Oliver!*, *Joseph and the Amazing Technicolor Dreamcoat*, *Jesus Christ Superstar* and *Grease*. In those days I wanted to be an actor, and I dreamed of playing the Artful Dodger. Oddly enough it never occurred to me I couldn't on account of my gender. We had a large dressing-up box and were endlessly putting on plays and entertainments for the many unsuspecting rectory visitors. I loved the drama of some church ceremonies, and the Easter story is one of the best, regardless of whether or not you believe it. Though my sister had a much better voice, I fooled around with what I believed was a highly amusing 'opera singer's wobble' (I called it 'wobble' not 'warble'). Long before my teenage years, this ability to throw myself into full-on performing all but vanished, though I longed for it. I am sure part of this shyness and anxiety at performing was due to the trauma of my father's death and the inevitable change in family circumstances. Throughout the rest of my school years, theatre was something I participated in only on the periphery – providing the soundtracks for the seemingly ultra-confident actors and singers among my peers. I yearned to be the onstage performer, but I had blockaded myself into more cerebral music-making.

A far safer form of singing was the rich world of choral music. I sang in excellent school choirs, and from university I was starting to conduct them. When I moved to London, I joined the London Philharmonic Choir and later the Philharmonia Chorus, not only for the repertoire but also to be under the baton of some of the great conductors of the late twentieth century – Lorin Maazel, Günter Wand and David Willcocks to name but a few. I didn't have a great instrument, but a reliable sight-singer has their uses in most choirs.

I had a friend in the chorus of English National Opera who got me £10 tickets to performances, and a few years on from my Glyndebourne experience, I was relieved to discover

I could follow the plots. Helped also by John Warrack's inspirational teaching, I was beginning to understand the powerful and subtle sounds, and opera was speaking to me as nothing else. It was through my boyfriend at the time that I was given a glimpse of how the whole thing was put together. Duncan Hinnells was one of a small group of university friends who wanted to become a conductor. He has ended up with a high-powered career in the law, but at that time he was forging ahead in music and getting some opportunities to dip his toe into opera conducting. I could see how attractive and immersive the rehearsal process was, and I was struck by what colourful characters these opera singers were. It wasn't just the dangerously attractive larger-than-life women he was working with that piqued my jealousy. They seemed to be having so much fun creating this musical drama. It was to be a few more years before I properly fell in love with this art form, and many years of hard work, coming up through the ranks and learning to decipher 'opera'.

Behind the Scenes

It was the long rehearsal process, from the studio to the theatre that helped me get to grips with it. We, the company, are living with this one opera for weeks on end, and the intensity of this compared with putting on a concert is seductive. An opera is expensive to produce because it involves so many disciplines, and this takes time as well as money. There are a few national and local differences, but there's a basic process that is pretty much universal, no matter the size of the production.

There's a creative team comprising stage director and set designer (and often a separate costume designer and lighting designer) who work closely together, and the conductor. Working alongside the stage director, there's often a movement director or choreographer, sometimes a fight director and occasionally in more recent years, an intimacy director. I think it's more helpful to see a conductor in an opera production as the music director. So, we have two directors, and this can be viewed as either an opportunity for rich collaboration, or for territorial battles. It's always the former for me, but it comes out of years of assisting and observing inspiring working practices as well as some disappointingly childish behaviour. For some the 'team player' role comes hard. On several occasions an assistant director and I have been forced to act as go-betweens when the directors were not talking to each other.

A music director will have a team of music staff, and this can be anything from one to even ten people. The essential and most unsung hero of opera in my opinion is the répétiteur. Rehearsal pianist, vocal coach, conductor's conscience, calm voice of reason, friend (for the duration of the rehearsal at least) – woe betide the conductor who doesn't value them! After the last performance of *Norma*, Calgary Opera held a party for Sandra Atkinson who was retiring after 48 seasons of working on the music staff there. In his speech Bramwell Tovey mused over why Sandy looked so young – an eighty-year-old who could easily pass for sixty: 'I think it's her smile.

The way she will look kindly at a conductor as if to say, "I know you've screwed up, but I won't tell anyone. How can I help you out of this?"'

Sometimes répétiteurs will share the rehearsal, but usually it's just one person and they will be at every rehearsal. In addition, there might be an assistant conductor, chorus master, language coach, offstage conductor and prompter. Depending on the size of the production and the budget, some of these jobs will be doubled up by the same person, and sometimes the répétiteur will be all the music staff in one. In very small productions the music director will also be the répétiteur and have no music staff. I am so lucky to have done all these jobs over the years and in many different places, covering a huge repertoire. This was my training. I am particularly glad of the ten years I spent working on at least one or two operas a year at the Royal Opera House. I might have been bottom of the food chain there, but I was working with the very best in the business and that rubbed off on me.

Prompting

My first job at Covent Garden was as a prompter. It is a dying skill, and I am one of the last conductors in the UK to get this brilliant opera conducting training. From 2005 to 2015 I usually prompted for at least one production a year, and I have witnessed some extraordinary musical and dramatic scenes both on and off the stage.

When learning an opera score, most conductors I know

will start by reading the libretto, and they constantly refer to the text, no matter how focused they are on musical matters. The drama and storytelling are everything – the dramatic structure and pacing, the shape, the rise and fall of a melody and phrase, this all relates to the text. I find if I am struggling to work out the right tempo for a section, I will usually get my answer from the text. The great composers of opera know exactly how to set words to music, which is an excellent argument for singing opera in its original language. Something is lost in translation. Having said that, I'm not the purist I used to be. If a foreign language interferes with communicating the story, particularly in fast-moving comedy, then I'm all for translating it into the native language of the audience, even if something is lost musically. Staging an opera always requires compromise, and opera can present so many barriers to the uninitiated. It can withstand compromises. Surtitles don't always help, and there's nothing worse than an audience glued to them instead of watching the stage. Delivering comprehensible translated text can be hard for singers, but worth it sometimes if it makes it more accessible. I have conducted Italian operas in English and Swedish, but I usually work in the original and early in my career I assisted many Italian conductors.

A conductor who doesn't know the libretto as well as the singers and the stage director will lack authority to direct and shape the music. Prompting allowed me to focus on this aspect of opera – the vocal line and an awareness of every breath and movement of a singer, of what they need from a conductor in a performance. It helped me to read singers.

I had learned to prompt at Gothenburg Opera, and when I returned to the UK in 2004, I emailed the Royal Opera House to ask if they ever needed a freelance prompter. An hour later the Head of Music, David Syrus, was on the phone, and within a few weeks I was booked for a production. In many European opera houses, particularly in Italy, Germany and Scandinavia, the prompter is still much in evidence. In the UK, the ROH is the only theatre that still has a prompt box, and even that is hidden away, only to emerge once or twice a year if that. The tradition used to be that all music staff (pianists, conductors, etc.) would start their professional lives as prompters. Edward Downes (former music director of the ROH) and Mark Elder spent a year or two in the box as young conductors, and it was considered an essential part of their apprenticeship training. Since the refurbishment in the new millennium, prompters are used only in emergency or with singers who, for various reasons, require it.

'What does a prompter do? Don't they just help out when a singer or actor forgets a line?' In fact, it's much more than that. Listen to old Maria Callas live recordings, and just a second before she sings a phrase, you might hear a voice speaking one or two words – a kind of spooky reverse echo. That's the prompter sitting in a box, at the front of the stage smack in the middle between the footlights. The tradition goes way back to the days before video and audio monitors. Most opera performances these days will have a camera on the conductor that is relayed via TV monitors hung quite high in the auditorium and in the wings – not visible to the audience. This allows the singers to keep contact with the conductor without always having to stare at them directly. There are also microphones picking up the sound from the pit, which is fed to the singers through speakers in the wings. This 'foldback' is needed because it's often very hard for singers to hear the orchestra, and in big theatres there can be a split-second delay in them hearing the sound from the pit. If they go with that delay, they won't sound together to the audience. Seated between the two, the prompter is that go-between from the pit to the stage.

There's more to the job than just shouting out a few words now and then, and the help needs to be tailored to the individual. Many singers will expect the prompter to deliver words before every single phrase, as an aide-memoire. To avoid singers coming in early, the universal hand sign for stop ('Speak to the hand!') comes in useful, then at exactly the right moment the prompter conducts them in with the hand and breath, mouthing the words. Some singers like the words to be mouthed all the way through – sometimes slightly ahead. Some singers are excellent lip readers, and I find wearing bright lipstick helps. I had an advantage over Sir Mark or Sir Edward there. Occasionally I have had to sing notes for singers, indicate with my hands when the melody is going up or down, even move them from note to note, cut off notes and mime words. An army salute mime before the word '*presenti*' was all one singer needed to get them started on a phrase. I have been known to quietly deliver stage directions – 'Ring the bell . . . now!' – or mime the precise moment of a stabbing. I rarely work with young children, but when I conducted a group of primary schoolchildren who had never sung with an orchestra before, it felt incredibly like prompting some of the most famous singers in the world.

One time a singer had to stand on the prompt box as part of the staging, and because they could neither see nor hear me, I gave cues by bashing on the roof of the box with my fist. 'Just prompt me when I look at you. The rest of the time I won't need it.' Prompters dread hearing that instruction. A bit of mind-reading is required for this, but the stress of keeping an eye on a singer who might suddenly need help is harder than assuming they need help all the time.

I must be very careful how loudly I speak the text. If the orchestra is loud, then I can and will need to shout. In quieter passages, to avoid being heard by the audience, I might have to rely on well-spat consonants. Usually, one or two words are sufficient, but occasionally in rehearsal and even performances I have had to give whole sentences – very rapidly. That's hard. Audiences rarely hear the prompter, but we are unpopular with BBC Radio 3 producers, especially if they have a microphone positioned near the box. Orchestras unused to it can find this additional noise distracting, and hate the space it takes up in their already cramped pit. Modern prompt boxes are often stored under the stage and, like a stair lift, rise out of the pit floor at the touch of a button. It's quite comfortable in there with a music stand and TV monitor showing the conductor. I got stuck once, when the box wouldn't go down, and the stage manager had to pull me out of the little hole during a break in the rehearsal. The ROH prompt box is open at the bottom, so my legs and feet are visible to players at the back of the pit – percussionists mostly. They have been known to try to pull my shoes off.

Most singers today are utterly appalled at the unprofessionalism of singers requiring prompting – especially in the UK where there is no tradition of this. I'm not so harsh a judge. If a singer from that European tradition uses a prompter, it doesn't mean they don't know the music. In emergencies a singer might be flown in at the last minute to replace someone, and a prompter can be their lifeline. On one occasion, I noticed a singer making their Covent Garden debut who'd had no memory problems in rehearsal suddenly go blank on opening night – a rabbit in the headlights. Although I was principally there to help another singer, I was able to take him through the show. Only he and I knew what had happened, and he gave me a big hug afterwards.

Singers who are unfamiliar with prompters will not want any help from me, and if I do give them a word, they think they must have gone wrong. Rarely will everyone in the cast need me, and in a complicated ensemble when they are all singing different parts with different entries, it can be tough. It's also quite annoying for the director who notices the singers gathering round centre stage, staring down. Sometimes the conductor will be happy to let the prompter cue all the singers' entries so they can focus on the orchestra. A

colleague of mine at the ROH told me of a moment early in
his career in the 1970s, when everyone used the prompter.
He realised his power as he brought the whole sixty-strong
chorus in a beat early.

There is usually a good deal of tension around in rehearsals because the singers that demand a prompter tend to be
rather famous. On one occasion a singer brought their own
coach, who prompted during the studio rehearsals, despite
my being the official prompter for the production. No one
dared tell him not to, and I knew the singer would need to
trust me to get through the performances. My only course
of action was to prompt louder than the coach, resulting in
a 'prompt off'. After about thirty minutes I won, and the
coach gave up and sat silently for the rest of the rehearsal.
This singer did trust me, and on that occasion I know the
performances would have ground to a halt without me. I
got a mention (not by name) in most of the reviews and
some of the chorus jokingly tried to bribe me to shout 'Kit
Kat' and see if the singer would copy me. Naturally I refused their offer.

Almost without exception I have had very pleasant working relations with singers I have prompted, who are nearly
always appreciative and polite. I did once lose my temper
with a singer who claimed I was too quiet in rehearsals. It
was strange because I was so loud I could be heard by the
chorus in the wings and the music staff at the back of the
auditorium, yet apparently I was too quiet for the singer who
was two feet away. The singer continued to bully me through

the rehearsal, and every time they went wrong, blamed me for being too quiet. What I eventually shouted at them is unrepeatable, but after that they were very friendly to me, and curiously their hearing suddenly returned. The chorus bought me a box of chocolates that day.

I have had some truly wonderful musical experiences in that prompt box. Sitting right in the heart of the sound, at times inches away from some of the greatest singers in the world, watching and feeling their whole bodies and spirits engaged in the drama and producing the most exquisite and thrilling sounds a human could ever make. Then below me, around me, feeling and hearing this world-class orchestra, and watching the great opera conductors of our time guide the gigantic ship that is an opera performance.

The Apprentice

Learning from the very best while building up my conducting experience in smaller companies was an excellent training. I know these apprenticeship years have made me a far better and more empathetic opera conductor. Similarly, Jane Glover joined the music staff at Glyndebourne in the late 1970s, and one of her main jobs was assisting Bernard Haitink. There are few better conductors, and that's where she learned her trade. She considers Glyndebourne her second alma mater after Oxford.

One of the first conductors I prompted for at the ROH was Antonio Pappano and I learned so much from watching him at work. He needed no introduction nor formal training in opera. It was in his DNA, and his journey to becoming one of the greatest conductors in this field was long and intense.

ANTONIO PAPPANO: In the early 1980s I got a répétiteur position at New York City Opera. This led me to working with singers who would tell me I should conduct because I played like an orchestra. And very slowly I was given opportunities. I worked with a big star in Denmark, Inga Nielsen. She brought me to the provinces there where she performed gala concerts, and I started conducting. I wasn't focused on technique, having not learned to conduct – shall we say – 'properly'. Although I think people saw there was some raw talent, I don't think the orchestra knew where to look, as my face was probably more communicative than my hands. But they invited me back, and I began to conduct symphonic repertoire – sometimes playing a Mozart piano concerto and conducting from the piano. It was conducting my first opera in Oslo (*La Bohème*) when I discovered what I was. In the first staging rehearsal I just took over, telling everyone how to sing and to act. I was fascinated by theatre and how it all fitted together – how one could never be divorced from the other.

During those years he was also playing the piano in different major international houses – the Liceu in Barcelona, the Lyric Opera in Chicago, and then on to Bayreuth to assist Daniel Barenboim for many years. He was working on two continents as a pianist and just occasionally conducting, but his prime focus was the piano. Coming up through the ranks as an apprentice he took a traditional route for most conductors of opera in the twentieth century. Working under masters and great singers was the education.

Pre-rehearsal

Sometimes, before rehearsals start, a music director will have been involved in casting along with the stage director. They will certainly have had much correspondence with the company manager about scheduling rehearsals well in advance. Usually, the stage director will talk informally to the music director about their vision for the piece, perhaps showing models of the set. It should be the music director's job, very diplomatically, to flag up any concerns – for example, a fancy mask or hat that covers a singer's face might prevent them from being able to see and hear or might muffle their sound. With experienced 'creatives' this is rarely a problem, but it's good to be aware so singers feel supported, and costumes don't need to be changed at the last minute.

A meet-and-greet session will be the first time the whole team gathers. It's a relatively small world, so usually some people know each other, though that combination of creative team, cast, music staff and stage management probably won't have existed before. It's always an exciting and slightly nerve-racking day. Other interested parties involved in the production are usually in attendance. Often seated in a circle, everyone takes it in turn to introduce themselves and their role: 'Hi! My name is ——— . . . and I'm an alcoholic.' *Joke . . . nervous laughter . . .* 'I'm playing the role of ———.' The stage director and his team will then talk about their vision and concept, showing a model of the set and photos of the costumes. In Sweden, the conductor is expected to talk about their interpretation as well, but in most places, they sit quietly and listen.

Leading up to the meet and greet, all of us will have been beavering away so we are all ready to play our part in the rehearsal process. Learning an opera score I find a lengthy business, even with one I've learned before.

Score Preparation

This is very personal, but here's what I do with an opera I've never conducted before, after years of trial and error. A standard opera score is a huge tome, so for me the key is not to be overwhelmed. There are usually whole sections or at least a few famous arias that I already know. Sometimes I have worked on it before as a member of the music staff but not conducted it. At the very least I've probably seen it performed but, whatever my knowledge, I prefer to start from scratch.

— I start with the libretto – text only and no music.
   If it's not in English, then I make sure I am able to

pronounce every single word and understand every idiom. Sometimes this includes referring to a good word-for-word translation with the International Phonetic Alphabet transliterations.

— I sit at the piano with a vocal score (a piano realisation, not the full orchestra version) playing it scene by scene many times, so it gets into my fingers and ears, and the harmonic progressions begin to flow.

— I learn each part role by role – almost as if preparing the role to sing myself. I find this useful because I follow each singer's journey. I notice difficult sections or when a singer is very busy in one scene and might be getting vocally tired, or when they haven't sung for a while, and might need a cue. I usually start with the larger roles and end with the chorus parts. Using coloured pencils, I mark every entry in the score – with the first letters of their name. I've done this for over twenty years: the sopranos will be shades of red; mezzos – orange; tenors – green; baritones – blue; basses – brown. The chorus is marked with fluorescent pens of pink, orange, green and blue. Some people would never dream of using coloured pens, but I know conductors and répétiteurs who do the same as me, using their own personal colour codes. This can be confusing if you suddenly need to borrow their score.

— That's just the vocal lines. I must delve right into the orchestral writing in the full score. Just as with learning a symphony I will carefully study the orchestral writing, working out who plays where. The difference is that I always have a thought for the vocal line and text.

— If it is a well-known opera, I listen to as many recordings as I can get my hands on. I might also watch videos of productions. I notice that live recordings of opera are sometimes slightly faster and often take more realistic tempi. It's all very well to indulge in a luxuriously slow tempo in the recording studio for the famous 'Casta Diva' aria in *Norma,* but in the show itself, it's the first thing Norma sings, and she has a lot more to do before she dies. Videos of live performances are also useful. I never stick to one recording. It is an excellent way of understanding the performance traditions and gives you ballpark ideas for tempi. Performance styles change over the decades, so it's always good to hear a mix. It's even useful to hear the less good recordings, because that's when you appreciate the problems you might encounter.

— It's then that I start looking at the orchestral writing in even more imaginative detail. I need a good knowledge of the drama and pacing that will inform every decision I make for the orchestra.

— I work out how I will wave my hands around, so I am clear to the singers and pianist. At this stage I don't have to spend as much time on this as I would preparing for a symphony orchestra rehearsal. I am about to repeat every scene many times in rehearsals before I meet the orchestra, and I'll soon find out what works and what doesn't.

This all takes time, and I try to do this over as long a period as possible, while working on other projects. Even with scores I have learned before, I like to start again (albeit at a much faster pace), and this is a real treat for me. I often buy a new score if it's not too expensive, so I can mark it up again. The process can help with the learning, and sometimes I look back on scores I marked up when I was younger and wonder what on earth was going through my head. There's so much operatic repertoire out there that I rarely conduct something twice. But there's always an opportunity to go deeper.

ANTONIO PAPPANO: In a few months I conduct *Rigoletto*, which will be the first time since 1991 [the performances took place in 2021]. Though I know every note and every word of that piece, having played it so many times as a répétiteur, I will relearn and reimagine it. I could look at it for an hour and go to the first rehearsal, not even having seen it for a long time, and it would be fine. But that's not the point. I want to make sure I know what every word means, and to start thinking about the accompaniment. I will dip in and out of the score over the next few months.

Rehearsals

These usually start with music alone – and last anything

from a day to a week. The music director and staff work through the whole opera. All the singers will be expected to come knowing their part, and how they interact with the rest of the cast. Singers will probably have worked with a coach on their role and if they're lucky with some of their colleagues, but usually this is the first time they will all have sung together. The music director's job is to make sure everything is musically secure before the singers are expected to start acting and moving around the room. I like the drama and storytelling to be at the heart of this process. If there's a chorus, then either the assistant conductor or chorus master prepares them in another room before they meet the music director. Sometimes the chorus is working on several operas simultaneously.

My first paid and the only full-time salaried job I have had was as chorus master at Gothenburg Opera. Soon after studying in Russia, I needed the money, and it was a good introduction to working in a large theatre, with a full-time company. It was a steep but fruitful learning curve in how to work with that very special group dynamic – a professional opera chorus. It changes surprisingly little from house to house, and country to country. Competition for a full-time position in a chorus is fierce – auditions attract international applicants. They are all well trained, some will go on to solo careers; some choose (or life chooses for them) to stay in the chorus – sometimes for decades or their whole professional lives. Many will have opportunities to sing small roles or cover larger roles as well, and many thrive in this environment. A steady income for an opera singer is not to be sneezed at. They are often treated as one group, but they are made up of individuals each with their own sense of artistry, and navigating that as a young professional chorus master is tough. Twenty years on, I cringe when I think of some of the managerial blunders I made with this group, but the artistic paybacks were rewarding too.

Operas comprise ensembles – anything from duets, trios, quartets, to larger groups of up to about ten soloists and a sixty-strong chorus. There's also recitative. This is sung and, coming between ensembles and arias, it has more the rhythm and pacing of normal speech and is more conversational. In Mozart's time this was either *accompagnato* (accompanied by the orchestra and therefore conducted) or *secco* (accompanied by a harpsichord, which always used to be and sometimes still is played by the music director). *Secco recit.* is not conducted, but the music director should be involved in the musical pacing of this alongside the stage director. Solo arias are usually the most famous tunes from the operas and are often performed separately and not just in the concert hall. Here the role of the music director should be subtle. Arias are not only opportunities for the soloist to show off their technical brilliance – they are also personal and highly expressive monologues. A singer might well have learnt the arias for years before the rest of a role. They usually know what works for them technically in terms of where they need to breathe and what tempo they can sing at. I love to hear what singers bring to this and, depending on their level of experience with different conductors, they will – I hope – come ready to give their version with confidence. There is always much to discuss between conductors and soloists, but if it fits with the dramatic pacing, is well thought through, and true to what's written on the page, then I'm all for not messing too much with it. Listening and supporting are key.

Stage Directors

After the music rehearsals, there follow around four or five weeks of full-time studio rehearsals. Actors will be familiar with the word 'blocking', which forms the early part of this process. Crudely put, the stage director works out where and how the singers move around the stage. It is much more than that of course and, even in the early stages, it's all part of the gradual creation of the drama. Ideally the music director will be at every rehearsal. Sometimes it might feel as though the work the stage director is doing is irrelevant to the music, but I've seen this attitude be the root of many a misunderstanding and squabble between these two leaders.

Stage directors vary in their rehearsal approach: some like to work in bite-size sections; some focus on character development in the early stages before running large sections in a more improvisatory fashion. Some get an overall outline done quickly in a week or so, returning to the beginning, shifting and tweaking, or indeed changing everything. When the production has already been performed elsewhere, then not so much devising and exploration needs to be done. The stage director then has a fully formed and already executed vision, and while they might change certain things to suit a new cast, or because they want to try a new angle, it is usually a more straightforward process and can be a shorter rehearsal period. Sometimes, with busy stage directors, a revival director or in permanent houses a staff director will be entrusted to this job. They had probably worked with the stage director on the original production.

Stage directors come in many shapes and sizes – some from 'straight theatre', moving into opera or combining the two. Coming from different backgrounds with degrees in all sorts of subjects (including music, English or drama), most can at least read music. Some have previously trained and worked as stage managers. There's only one place in the UK where you can study for a full-time master's in opera directing (at the Royal Welsh College of Music & Drama) and that course is only a few years old. Many learn their craft by a combination of assisting directors and staging their own operas, some even starting their own companies. Parallels are often drawn with conductors, and they might share personality traits – hence the squabbling. Sadly, access and inclusivity to this profession is similarly limited. Until recently, women were vastly under-represented, and still the gender statistics are shamefully bad in big opera houses around the world. Seeing the number of talented young female stage directors makes me cautiously optimistic for the future, provided they are not filtered out in their progression up the career ladder.

Whatever the stage director's style, the music should always be at the heart of the process. Usually before they start to block a scene, the music director will 'run it musically' and this is often the first time the stage director has heard the cast singing it. It's a good moment for the music director to rehearse a bit. It might have been a while since their music rehearsals and things get forgotten, but I am mindful that this time is precious for staging. In my apprenticeship years, I'd sometimes witness a conductor take over for way too long, oblivious to (or deliberately ignoring) the anxious stage director looking at their watch. Once I've run a scene and corrected mistakes where necessary, I am always keen to involve the stage director. This is particularly important in recitative, and many fascinating conversations on pacing and dramatic flow come out of this time.

ANTONIO PAPPANO: The best advice I can give to a conductor is: 'Never switch off in the rehearsal room. Always listen to what's going on – when the director stops to fix things or talk about nuance and character.' Because that's something you can enhance with the music, the temperature – getting the music to embrace the subtle expressions that the director and singers are searching for.

Essentially this is staging time, and the music director and répétiteur are there to provide the musical support so that every time the singers sing and act, they have accompaniment and a conductor they can lock into. Finding out places where they will need to connect to the conductor to ensure they will be together with the orchestra is an important but subtle process. An experienced music director and singer will quickly figure out places where the conductor must lead, where the singer is allowed more space, or where they just need an understanding between them. A certain amount of consistency and mutual trust is important, and this is built up in the studio during these weeks. Once on the stage, the singers will be able to see the conductor not just in the pit, but via TV monitors out in the auditorium. In the early days of switching from analogue to digital there were problems with time delays (the monitor conductor appeared to be behind the real one), but now this has largely been ironed out.

We have come a long way from the traditional idea of 'park and bark' opera, where a singer waddles onto the stage and delivers – with almost no acting. Nothing can irritate those of us who work in this genre more than to hear the outdated adage: 'Opera singers can't act.' This usually comes from a person who has actually not seen an opera in a good few years (or ever), or who has had one or two bad experiences and is willing to lump all opera singers into this group. I have conducted operas in some of the UK's top conservatoires, and while I can see some singers have a more natural acting talent than others, they all get a decent training. The stage directors they work with are at the top of their game too and demand the very highest levels, preparing them to enter the profession. Operas are nearly always musically complex and vocally demanding, requiring extreme stamina. A singer who can trot out a famous three-minute opera aria with some success might not necessarily be able to sing the rest of the opera, which rarely lasts less than two hours. Unamplified, they need to produce a beautiful sound that cuts through the orchestra and hits the back of the auditorium. They do all this often in a language that's not their mother tongue, while running round the stage, acting their hearts out. Sometimes stage directors will deliberately ask them to act against the music, and this can work well, heightening the music in contrast and adding a level of dramatic tension. This is a challenge and can play havoc with the most rhythmic of singers, but usually it can be achieved by good rehearsal techniques, and a patient and supportive yet demanding stage director. Something that wasn't possible during social distancing, and that I really missed, was having a quiet word with a singer, out of earshot of their colleagues – not always pointing out mistakes in public. This gentle form of rehearsing goes on right the way through the process, even once the performances are up and running. It is important if singers are not to feel picked on. Their instrument is their body, and any criticism can feel very personal.

Singers need to build up stamina for a large role, especially if they haven't done it before. The rehearsal period can be tough on their vocal cords and experienced singers will know when to 'mark' in rehearsal – to sing more quietly and at a more comfortable octave. There's an art to good marking and knowing when to employ it, because singers still need to sing with energy and with musical and dramatic intention. Sometimes singers feel pressure to impress all the time, and don't mark enough. It's good for a music director to encourage judicial marking, and not let them burn out before opening night.

Singers will need to use their peripheral vision or look directly at the conductor. If they are well prepared, rhythmically strong, the phrase is flowing and the tempo is regular, they can go about their business on stage without needing to look directly at the conductor all the time. There is a thread of contact between the two, but it's not always visible. I don't enjoy watching operas where the singers seem utterly glued to the conductor. Not only does it look dramatically boring, but I think it gives the audience a sense of unease and they are more likely to notice something going wrong. And things do go wrong all the time in live opera. Singers can accidently go 'off piste', just a tiny bit or massively so. The degree of the catastrophe will have as much to do with how the music director spent their time in those early rehearsals as it does with how they respond in the performing moment.

Some stage directors see their role as a boundary breaker, challenging the art form, while others are more conservative, but both can be equally demanding of their singers. The music director is wise to keep an open and supportive attitude to both types. Criticising the production to the singers (this has been known to happen and usually behind the stage director's back) will not help. Even if they are right and the concept isn't working at all, it will do nothing but make the already nervous singers even more insecure. That's why

I believe collaboration and communication is at the heart of this job. Music directors are focused on trying to reproduce what's on the page in a living, breathing performance and being true to the composer. On the other hand, the public and critics expect stage directors to be original – a tough call with the popular mainstream repertoire. Yet they are all too ready to criticise when that originality is taken too far. I admire and do not envy the stage director.

So, in these crucial stage rehearsals the two directors should be mutually supportive, which can include respectfully challenging each other's ideas. They keep an eye and ear on the singers from different perspectives but should be completely aware of what the other is asking for. That doesn't mean they have to agree with each other all the time, but open and constructive discussion, which doesn't take too long and bore the singers, is a good thing. Personally, I've nearly always found this to be an extremely positive and rewarding experience, where ideas feed off each other. Conducting is a lonely job and I welcome sharing the responsibility of leadership.

The Orchestra

Towards the end of this period, the music director will disappear for a few days, leaving the assistant conductor and répétiteur in charge, while they meet the orchestra for the first time. Depending on the budget, length and technical difficulty of the opera, or if the orchestra has played it before, there are usually at least three 'orchestra alone' rehearsals.

In Good Hands

The orchestra won't know anything about the production, unless some or all of them are going to appear on stage, and have been involved in costume fittings. In many ways, these rehearsals are the same as rehearsing for a concert, except for the obvious fact that the singers are absent, so it doesn't sound complete. There's a danger these rehearsals can be a bit dull, so I like to start making music straight away. Orchestras don't like long speeches but, as we work through the scenes, I explain the story. Very often, the orchestra is in the pit, so most of them won't be able to see the stage. Some will know the synopsis of old, some will have read it beforehand, and listened to recordings or videos, but it's not a given. It's good to keep the rehearsal as lively and inspiring as possible, and with the voices missing, it sometimes doesn't make much sense.

ANTONIO PAPPANO: I'm notoriously bad at telling the stories of opera, which are often totally preposterous anyway, but I always attempt an encapsulated version for the orchestra. I'm not making them up, but when I cut to the chase, they do become very funny. I do it partly to stimulate the collective emotional intelligence of the orchestra, which is a wonder to behold. The love triangles, jealousy, mistaken identity – the stuff that is sometimes the essence of Italian opera – is funny, but also painful and emotional, and the orchestra knows that. Approaching something that's very serious with humour can be an antidote. I live most of my life in tragic opera stories, and it helps to find that levity, to offset the serious business of making the music.

Conductors sometimes need to sing in phrases – loudly and unapologetically. I'm no opera singer, and I'm just giving them helpful cues. But if you sing too loudly, you don't allow yourself to hear the orchestra properly, which is your main job. I use my singing voice sparingly, and recently I found it better to sing very little in these rehearsals.

In standard repertoire, players in an experienced opera orchestra (as opposed to those who predominantly play concert repertoire) will already be aware of the danger moments, where things can easily fall apart. They will also know the traditions – for example, in some places where the soprano or tenor has a very high note, it's expected that the orchestra will hold the chord to allow them to show off their spectacular sound before ending the phrase. This is usually for dramatic and musical emphasis and not just vocal acrobatics. Sometimes this is written into the score and their parts, and sometimes it's a stylistic tradition handed down through generations. A decision might be made not to hang around at some of these moments, and the music director needs to let the orchestra know all this. Pencils and marking of parts are essential.

An ideal schedule will allow the music director to return to the production studio for a studio run. This is when the whole opera is performed with piano, and most of the props. Many of those who were at the meet and greet will see it for the first time. Notes for the singers will be given afterwards

– musical and dramatic, and we are ready for the next stage.

The singers and orchestra meet for the first time in what's called a *Sitzprobe*, which is German for a 'seated rehearsal'. The focus is purely and simply on the music. In an ideal world it will take place on the stage with the orchestra in the pit, and I know some conductors who prefer to make this a semi-staged rehearsal, allowing the singers to move around as they will later. That's useful if rehearsal time is very limited, but I prefer to go back to the score, to focus on one thing only before the lights, costumes and everything else arrive. If a singer has never sung their role before, or if it is a new opera, this will be the first time they are to be accompanied by the whole orchestra, and while the music is enhancing, it can be unsettling. The répétiteur will have been reproducing the orchestra, as far as humanly possible, but the sound world is going to be very new and could be unnerving for less experienced singers. The music director, who had previously been focusing almost entirely on the singers, will have many more things to hold together and will usually be further away. Ideally there is time to rehearse and repeat sections, but sometimes it's not even possible to play the whole opera. The rest of the music staff will be listening hard and making notes that will later be relayed to interested parties.

Onstage

We are on stage now for the stage-and-piano or technical rehearsals. These can be scheduled for anything from two days to a week. In all the years I've been working in opera, the first S&P almost never starts on time. Or rather it does, but from where the music staff and director are standing it appears not to have done. Complicated technical things need to be in place before the music starts, and most of that happens behind the scenes, invisible to us. These are the stage director's rehearsals, and the music director's job is to sit quietly in the pit and wait for the stage manager to tell them when to start and stop conducting. I rather enjoy this time, feeling as it does a bit like the calm before the storm. A moment for me to recharge while the stage director becomes slightly panicked. Once we begin to run scenes, or rather stagger through them with many stops and starts, the music director and staff will have their ears alert ready to make copious notes. We find moments later to give corrections to the singers, after figuring out if the mistake was something they needed to be aware of or was simply because they were simultaneously dealing with a costume issue or trying to open a stuck door. Occasionally I might stop a rehearsal to correct something because it is clearly so problematic that leaving it be will only create problems later down the line but, overall, it's important to respect that this is the stage director's time. Ideally we get to do an 'S&P' dress rehearsal with wigs, make-up and costumes.

The music director's time comes when the orchestra returns for the 'Stage & Orchestra' rehearsals, and the stage director hands over the reins. The latter is watching and making notes they discreetly relay to singers, but they take a back seat. With luck, all the technical and dramatic aspects of the opera will have been ironed out and we can enjoy putting this last bit of the jigsaw together. There's usually a similar amount of time as for the S&Ps, and I think the emphasis at this point is to start running very large sections or whole acts, and then to return to the places that nearly (or actually) fell apart. However, it is important for the music director to be aware that they can't just start exactly where they want to and expect all that's happening on stage to work immediately. Stage managers like to know the general outline of the rehearsal, so they can prepare their technical team to stand by either to return to an earlier scene or to go on. Sometimes there are moments where a scene change will mean nothing can happen on stage for a few minutes, but this is never wasted time, as the music director can give notes to the orchestra or singers if they are available.

All these stage rehearsals are for the technical team as well, and scene changes speed up as they are repeated. A music director who doesn't understand this and starts complaining about slow changes is tiresome for the stage manager but, due to the opera hierarchy, unfortunately they must bite their tongue and smile politely at the 'maestro'.

The podium is about the worst possible place for hearing anything. The orchestra is loud and it's hard to hear the singers, so this is when the music director will rely on their staff. They will be seated in different places, but usually the assistant conductor will be just behind the conductor so they can converse easily. A conductor I assisted once unhelpfully shouted at me in one of these rehearsals, 'Why she make horrible noise?' It's worth remembering it's not only the orchestra sound that the foldback microphones pick up and relay to the singers on stage. I didn't take that aspect of his rehearsing technique with me into my career.

It's important for someone to be listening far out in the auditorium and trying different seats. The biggest balance issues are with the orchestra overpowering the singers, and the music staff needs to indicate specific places where the volume should be kept lower. An assistant conductor will also be listening out for balance and other issues within the orchestra itself. This will all be relayed back to the music director. The répétiteur will be making notes of singers' mistakes and the language coach will be doing their bit. Notes are usually given between rehearsals or emailed out.

Throughout this process, the conductor is working at a very practical level, bringing everything together, but also in many subtle ways aiming to lift the performance to higher artistic levels.

Offstage

In many operas there is music that happens offstage – from one singer sounding as if they are in another room, or about to enter, to a whole band of about twenty instrumentalists and a full chorus. Some productions require more than one off-stage conductor to give a truly multi-directional sound and to allow time to move around the theatre between cues.

For example, in *Lohengrin* at the Royal Opera House, four conductors are needed. Only the very biggest and richest of houses can afford that luxury. Offstage conducting is an art in itself, thankless, and noticeable only when it goes wrong. Depending on the size of the theatre and exactly where the offstage conductor is positioned, there will be a time lag with the orchestra in the pit, and a slightly narrower time lag with the singers on the stage. Before the technological support of modern times, I can only imagine these moments often sounded messy. How much support is available is dependent on the budget. Ideally the offstage conductor will have a set of headphones and a speaker relaying the sound from the pit with no time lag. They will also be able to hear the slightly later sound coming from the pit, from the stage, and of course from the band in front of them. That's three separate time streams. There will also be a TV monitor showing the music director and it is important to be glued to this, although for all the different groups to sound together out in the auditorium, the offstage conductor's beat will have to be slightly ahead. The band members will have very little information (perhaps a sound monitor) and will have arrived just five minutes or so before they are due to play. Sometimes they make one appearance for a few minutes of music, and sometimes many more appearances and for longer. The offstage conductor therefore needs a countdown both vocally and with their hands. Normally it's the job of the offstage conductor to rehearse the band. The sensation of offstage conducting I can only liken to playing the organ in a large church with a choir or congregation far away. Ploughing on and not waiting for the sound is essential. You know when it works, but you can't say how.

Those of us lucky enough to have done this job will have many stories of mishaps – TV monitors breaking down, or the instrumentalists lost in another part of the building. On one occasion, after I'd rehearsed the band, five out of six trumpeters had gone for a late breakfast and missed their call to return for the run-through. Another time, in an outdoor park theatre, I had two minutes to move from conducting singers in the wings to conducting a brass band at the back of the auditorium. One night I discovered the park gate was locked, and I had to run around the other way, arriving out of breath and two minutes late. The band didn't play that night. Fortunately, the music director, Peter Robinson, who had done plenty of offstage work in his time, was completely understanding, and slightly amused. That's why it's so important for young conductors to experience these behind-the-scenes jobs, so they don't throw a hissy fit when it occasionally goes wrong. It's not the most artistic of roles, it is often stressful, but I found it strangely satisfying when it all worked, which was surprisingly often.

Finale

Back to the pit. Like many conductors, I find the post-it note a useful tool because while conducting, I don't have a spare hand to make notes. I tear them into small pieces and stick them around the stand, so when I hear something that I know needs correcting, I'll quickly grab one and slap it down on the offending bar. I have time then to go back at the end or after the rehearsal, and just seeing the yellow note is enough to remind me of what went wrong. I use them in the studio rehearsal, and sometimes I even have a few handy in a run of performances. By the end of the rehearsal period, with bits of colourful paper strewn around like wedding confetti, my podium resembles the outside of a church door on a Saturday afternoon.

If we're lucky, then there will have been opportunities to run the whole opera at least once in the S&O period, because the dress rehearsal, sometimes called the general rehearsal, is basically a performance. The directors reserve the right to stop, and the singers can mark, especially if their opening night is the next day, but very often an audience is invited to attend. There's a buzz about this, but if things have gone well up until then, there should be a sense of calm too. The hardest part of the job has been done, and the performing can begin. The music director's job now is to drive the show, to be consistent, alert and ready to react and shift at any given moment, and along with all the performers ensure every show has fresh energy.

Out of the Pit

For centuries the proscenium tradition of a stage, pit and audience has been the norm for opera, ballet and musicals.

As orchestral forces for both opera and ballet have increased, the size and depth of the pit has also grown, and the gap between audience and singers can be huge. In recent years I have worked with smaller companies with reduced orchestras or new operas with bespoke chamber ensembles. Often the orchestra has been on the stage, usually at the back or the side, but still visible to the audience. The singers can see me on TV monitors, so they can face out to the audience. While I miss the eye-to-eye, breath-to-breath contact, in many ways I love this set-up. If I have rehearsed properly, it shouldn't present ensemble problems. There are almost never the balance issues of the orchestra overpowering the voices, and the audience has a more immediate connection with the singers.

Many stage directors have relished our presence on the stage and have included us in the drama. In a production called *Carmen Moves* at Folkoperan in Stockholm, the disciplines of 'dance' and 'opera' were fused. Combining Bizet's opera *Carmen* with the Soviet composer Rodion Shchedrin's ballet of the same name, not only did dancers and singers perform together, but the choreographer Örjan Andersson also included us in the dance. I was more nervous about dancing a waltz with the toreador Escamillo than any conducting, but it was great fun. Another clever way of interacting with the audience is the immersive promenade opera, where the performers move around a larger space alongside the audience, who move around with them. One of the most artistically rewarding productions I have ever done was Peter Maxwell

In Good Hands

Davies's *Kommilitonen!* at Welsh National Opera with their Youth Opera Company, directed by Polly Graham. A story of revolutionary students, this contemporary work was already musically challenging, and the ever-moving singers did nothing to make my life easier, but it was worth it.

Performances

One of the big pluses of working in a theatre is the number of repeat performances compared with the concert hall. It certainly helps the bank balance, since mostly we are paid per performance, even though preparing scores and rehearsing is often the most time-consuming bit. The performance fees reflect that, but nonetheless the more performances the merrier as far as I'm concerned. Something I have learned and improved on over the years is maintaining the energy level in a long run.

Multiple performances give an opportunity for assistant conductors to take over in the pit. Most of us have cut our teeth doing this, and it is a terrifying yet essential rite of passage.

A formative experience was in 2001 just after I had finished my studies, when I was an assistant conductor on a three-month USA tour of a production of *Carmen*. With seventy performances, a different theatre every night, 17,000 miles with the whole company in two coaches, the challenges were not just musical. There were marriages and divorces resulting from that tour. I played in the orchestra (keyboard and percussion) and conducted ten performances. I soon learned that unless you are properly committed to every show, you will get very bored very quickly.

More recently I conducted fifty-five performances within six months of Philip Glass's opera *Satyagraha*. The focus and concentration required for this long minimalist work was immense, and at the most intense period I was conducting it five days in a row several times over a period of a month. I did a similar number of performances of Puccini's dramatic work *Turandot*. They couldn't be more different, yet I found with both I needed to rest up a bit on performance days. It didn't stop me feeling guilty for working only in the evening, but earlier in my career I had ignored this need to be fresh, and I think the performances suffered.

Before each performance it's good to check in with the singers. Finding the right time to knock on their dressing-room door is sometimes a challenge. Costumes, wigs, make-up and warming up their voices – there's a lot of preparation for singers and you don't want to interrupt that, but you want to be there for them and make that connection before seeing them on stage. Taking them with you in the performance run, and not just the rehearsals, is important.

That's the basic framework of how an opera is put together and performed. There are of course variations to this, but it is surprising how little it changes. I find this quite comforting when I arrive in a new country, and while there are regional differences, the rehearsal schedule in Singapore is basically the same as in Canada or Malta.

Seventeenth to Twenty-first Century

Conductors became a necessity only as ensembles grew in size, and this is as true in opera as in other areas of classical music. Traditionally Baroque, Classical and early Romantic music would be led from the keyboard. These days we often have both a conductor and a harpsichordist, but there are some who do both. Versatile conductors such as Antonio Pappano will play and conduct (even operas as late as Rossini's *Il barbiere di Siviglia,* written in the early nineteenth century), but there are also those who specialise in early music, particularly opera. The 1970s saw an emergence of a new way of performing early music – or rather a return to the old way.

I had a bit of training in early performance practice on the organ, but my development as a conductor and where I feel most at home is in the Romantic repertoire – the very melodramatic, heart-on-sleeve stuff that puzzled me so in my teens. The earliest I dare go is Mozart, leaving brilliant people like Laurence Cummings to give energy and expertise to anything earlier. Mozart was the ultimate game-changer in the history of opera, and when I conduct his music, I see his influence in every operatic composer that followed, but for Laurence it's the other way round.

LAURENCE CUMMINGS: It's taken me until now to feel like I can tackle Mozart, and it's a joy because it feels very late and adventurous. For me, Mozart's genius lies in his ability to confound the listener's expectation. Coming fresh from earlier eighteenth-century repertoire I really experience it as a shock.

And then of course I do the classic seventeenth- and eighteenth-century harpsichord thing and skip to the twentieth and twenty-first centuries. I've conducted Stravinsky's *The Rake's Progress*, for example. Ironically this is when I got to dress up in period costume and fulfil my ambition to play the incredible harpsichord part.

Twentieth- and twenty-first-century opera includes every possible style and taste – from intimate chamber operas, with a handful of players and singers, to huge symphonic forces in the pit and sometimes more than sixty singers on the stage. The musical styles and subject matter vary too, from tunefully romantic comedies to gritty hard-hitting contemporary stories, and everything in between. There are orchestral reductions of classic operas, allowing them to be performed in smaller venues, or for the socially distanced requirements of a pandemic. Some works are site-specific, and not written for an opera house at all, dispensing entirely with the traditions of the pit and stage. At the other end of the scale from Laurence, composer and conductor Richard Baker specialises in conducting music that has only just been written, or is still in the composition process. The job is the same as for any opera music director, but often with much more contact with the composer, so it starts earlier in the creative process (see Chapter 9).

The Future

I have come a long way from my Glyndebourne experience over thirty years ago, and yet I still feel I have only just scratched the surface. I can't wait to see what exciting productions I will be involved in during the next thirty years. I hope the great traditions of opera will continue and flourish, but it's all for the good that the genre is evolving too. I look forward to seeing my colleagues around the world find new ways of making opera more inclusive, allowing a wider public to experience this great art form both as listeners and performers.

8: Ballet

Boredom

Nearly a decade before my first opera experience, my mother took me to a performance of the famous ballet *La Fille mal gardée* at the Theatre Royal, Norwich. I can't have been more than eight years of age, so I've no idea which of the wonderful UK companies it was. Yet I do have a very strong memory of the experience, and that was of utter boredom. As a clergy daughter, I had sat through enough sermons and services in my short life to recognise the feeling, but sermons are rarely more than ten minutes and services are usually done and dusted in an hour. This was two interminable hours long. At the time I was attending ballet classes and while I was not gifted in that area, I was quite keen for a while, mostly because of the child actors in the BBC series adapting Noel Streatfeild's book *Ballet Shoes*. As an adult I have sat in audiences surrounded by little girls and witnessed them be utterly transported into this magical world, so perhaps there was something wrong with me. Just as with the Glyndebourne experience, I think a bit of prepping would have helped. I loved stories and storytelling, but the language was too unfamiliar for me to follow.

It was two decades later in St Petersburg when I could finally begin to appreciate the art form, and what better place than the Mariinsky Theatre, formerly the Kirov? Not only was this home for many of the greatest dancers and choreographers of ballet history, but it was also where the French choreographer Marius Petipa first met and collaborated with Tchaikovsky. Watching and listening to *Nutcracker* or *Swan Lake*, and knowing it was first performed on that very stage, how could I not be drawn in? Tchaikovsky's music is in the walls and the very air of that building. There were plenty of opportunities to see Stravinsky's works too: *Le Sacre du printemps*, for example, was staged regularly. My favourite night out was to see Prokofiev's *Romeo and Juliet* (also premiered at the Mariinsky), and this was usually performed at least once a month.

I was lucky to be studying in a place where ballet was highly regarded in the musical establishment – at least the works of these three composers. But like many 'serious' classical musicians, I was late to the party.

Baptism of Fire

Barry Wordsworth, former Music Director of The Royal Ballet Covent Garden, explains the prejudice and ignorance that until recent decades permeated the classical music world:

Back in the 1970s, ballet was a dirty word. Going to the opera was acceptable, but when students attended the ballet, the response would be a bewildered, 'What did you do that for?' I think that's why there's such a stigma around it. So many conductors have tried it, didn't really know what they were doing, got shouted and screamed at, so they would think, 'Well, forget that!' And it's a shame because, as part of your life as a conductor, to be able to conduct in the theatre, be it opera or ballet, is a wonderful thing.

In recent years, ballet companies have worked harder at providing training and mentoring for young conductors, and now there are more opportunities in the major UK companies. Yet there's still a way to go, and there's some snobbery around conducting ballet.

For Barry it was purely by chance that he found himself in this world. He had just returned to London, having spent a year of study in Amsterdam with Bernard Haitink and Gustav Leonhardt. He had rather gone off the idea of conducting:

As far as I was concerned there were so many wonderful musicians who had become tainted by being conductors. They had either made it and become so grand they were on another planet, or they hadn't made it in the way they had hoped and had become terribly bitter. I decided to concentrate on the harpsichord because I loved playing continuo.

He was back in London and wondering what to do with his life:

I was actually decorating the dining room when the phone rang and someone from The Royal Ballet said, 'We understand you play the harpsichord. Do you know the Frank Martin Harpsichord Concerto?' The choreographer Kenneth MacMillan had made a ballet called *Las Hermanas* – based on Lorca's play *The House of Bernarda Alba* – and the harpsichordist was taken ill. I lied and said, 'Yes.' I had three days to find a copy and prepare it. I learned the first five pages of each movement, and the cadenza. I can remember the audition vividly. I got to page four and thought, 'Oh god! They are just going to let me play on.' But then, 'Thank you very much, Barry. Can you just play us a bit of the slow movement?' And the same thing happened again. So, they thought I knew it quite well. But then they said, 'You've got the job, and the performance is next week!' I only had a week to learn the whole thing.

With a combination of talent, youthful chutzpah and focused hard work, Barry pulled it off. The successful ballet stayed in the repertoire, allowing him to tour with the company as he began to understand this new theatre and ballet world:

Just going through the stage door at Sadler's Wells and seeing all the different disciplines – the wig department, the stage scenery. I was in heaven. I couldn't believe it.

Las Hermanas fell out of the repertoire, and his services were no longer needed. Then, a few weeks later, another phone call:

'We've just heard that you like conducting. Could you turn up at the Theatre Royal Brighton and conduct a matinee performance of *Solitaire*?' The music was Malcom Arnold's *English Country Dances*. I had no idea what I was doing but luckily I had friends in the orchestra. Their advice was: 'Do everything as you would in a concert, only slower!' As luck would have it, it went rather well, and at the end of the performance they said, 'Would you like the job of assistant conductor on tour?'

This was The Royal Ballet Touring Company which became Sadler's Wells Royal Ballet, and eventually Birmingham Royal Ballet.

I was tremendously lucky because John Auld as assistant director and then Sir Peter Wright who took over the company were such wonderful people. They helped me to understand what it was to be a ballet conductor.

I was conducting straight away, and we had a great team of musicians. We were all out on tour together, and we lived together. In those days the tours around the UK would last for twelve weeks. We played Monday to Saturday and travelled to the next town on Sunday – usually on the same train or on a coach.

I came to ballet much later in my career than Barry. I was in my mid-thirties, and by that time I was beginning to feel quite comfortable in theatre and had experienced a fair bit of podium time both in opera and symphonic repertoire. Over a period of about five years, I conducted productions with many of the major UK ballet companies. Alongside work with smaller touring opera companies and as a member of the music staff working with The Royal Opera, this experience conducting large orchestras was invaluable. Like Barry I was an assistant, and in most cases this meant getting performances on tour. This is the only way of learning, really experiencing it, a baptism of fire though it may be.

Quite early in this period, I conducted *Swan Lake* with Birmingham Royal Ballet. It's stunning music, and a joy to conduct, but also tough for the unseasoned ballet conductor. There are many tricky solos and ensembles, where getting that tempo right for the dancer is essential. An experienced first conductor, Philip Ellis, took all the orchestra and most of the stage rehearsals, and as second conductor I carefully observed him and the dancers, made notes on what speeds the dancers needed, was given a lot of invaluable advice and support, and then jumped in on about performance number four. No matter how good you are, how carefully you prepare, how well supported you are, your first performance is likely to have room for improvement. I practised conducting the ballet in the privacy of my hotel room at the Holiday Inn opposite the Birmingham Hippodrome – barely room to wave my arms. Unlike practising an instrument, I get no sound coming back at me. From experience and training I can have a very good idea of what the orchestra will sound like, depending on how I move my hands and arms, and I can practise starting different sections, and transitions into new sections, at the right tempi. But it's a bit like practising the piano on a table with no keys, or a violin with a bow, but no violin. The first time I was to play my instrument, in this case the orchestra, would be very public, and frightening.

The day before my first show, the stage manager bounded up to me. 'Hi, Alice! Sadly, I won't be there tomorrow as I've got an appointment at the dentist . . . ughh!' I actually felt jealous, and at that point I asked myself whether I might have chosen the wrong career. Would I seriously prefer root canal surgery to conducting this masterpiece with this fabulous orchestra? Well, yes! At that moment, *definitely* yes!

The performance wasn't quite as bad as I'd feared; no dancers were seriously harmed in the making of it and the orchestra seemed fairly content. I was given a short list of the tempi I hadn't quite nailed from the dancers' point of view, which is standard practice, even with more experienced conductors. The one glaring mistake was in 'The Spanish Dance'. I realised immediately as I looked up at the stage, but it was too late. Not quite setting the right tempo can sometimes be like missing the junction on a motorway. You must soldier on, there's no turning back or correcting until the next exit. As I took a fast tempo (that would have been fine in a concert), I forced a group of the *corps de ballet* not to look quite as graceful with their tambourines as usual and somewhat out of breath as they took their bows. I was quickly forgiven with good grace and humour, though I had to endure Philip teasingly calling it 'Doing an Alice' for the rest of the run. I was able to rectify everything the next day in my second show, and after that I began to look forward to every performance. The dentist's chair was no longer an attractive option. I was back to loving my job.

After a few years I was invited to be in charge as a guest conductor on some productions outside the UK, and every few years or so I get asked to conduct a ballet, a modern dance production or a hybrid version of the two. My most recent production was in 2022. *Swan Lake* with the brilliant French company Ballet Preljocaj was a very satisfying mix of the original score and some electronic additions. The challenge for me was that the company had performed to a recording for over two years, getting used to one fixed tempo throughout. But not for long, as everyone enjoyed the living organism of live music.

Language

Coming via opera, I could see that ballet was another language I needed to learn, yet there were similarities with opera, and this was fascinating to me. Both are theatre and both have a strong visual aspect, but with ballet it is all visual. Of course, music is essential to ballet, but if it doesn't look right, then it is wrong. With opera, if something isn't quite working visually, the music can carry the moment. The singer can lift the drama, the meaning of the music, with their voice alone. It's not ideal, but it can and does happen. Not so with ballet. The most sublime sounds can be emanating from the pit, but if the dancers are unable to fit the steps to music, then it won't work for the audience, and will be a horrible experience for the dancers. Just as an opera conductor connects with the singers, a ballet conductor must connect with the dancers. For example, if a conductor takes a tempo in an aria that's too fast for a singer, they can make them sound bad, and it is the same for a dancer.

> BARRY WORDSWORTH: The strange thing is that eyes and ears are terribly close. You really have to learn a different code to use your eyes in the same way that an opera conductor would use their ears.

A healthy dose of humility and empathy is important for both types of theatre conductor. It's all very well for a conductor to have a vision of how the music goes, but if it doesn't work for the singer or the dancer, they are the one who may end up falling flat on their face – metaphorically or even literally. The conductor hiding away in the pit must care about that.

In many ways, ballet conducting provides more challenges. The two essential elements, music and dance, must work together, yet dancers and musicians speak and read different languages. In opera, an orchestra can hear the singers, so although the conductor is steering the ship, the orchestra is also responding to what they hear on stage. Many an experienced opera orchestra has saved the bacon of the inexperienced conductor by staying longer on a note because they know the singer isn't about to move off it. In ballet, only the conductor can see the stage and the dancers. All the orchestra can hear is some very loud thudding above them, which couldn't be further removed from what we see on stage. Stravinsky's *Firebird* is nicknamed *Fire Elephant* by one well-known British ballet orchestra.

Just as in opera, performance traditions have been handed down through the centuries, and what's written in the score is not the whole story. What looks on paper to be a short note might be held for a long time because, for example, a dancer is being lifted and held in the air by another dancer at the climax of a *pas de deux*. At the climax of an aria a singer might stay up on a high note for a while, and as they come off the note and slide down (*portamento*), the conductor and orchestra will catch them at the bottom. Similarly, a ballet dancer might be held in the air by her partner, and as she moves to another position, the conductor will catch them and move to the next chord. The difference of course is that the orchestra can't hear that move, so they must trust the conductor.

BARRY WORDSWORTH: In ballet, you are the person who persuades them that you're not going mad. You do really mean to hold that note, and you can do it in a way that keeps their discipline and their respect for what they're doing a hundred per cent. That's why I love it.

Orchestras who are used to playing ballet come to know these places, and are ready to react quickly, and because it is live theatre, just like opera, the unexpected can happen. Orchestra and conductor alike are on high alert.

Notation

Singers and instrumentalists read the same musical notation. We are singing from the same hymn sheet so to speak, yet in most Western countries it is rare, though not unheard of, for dancers to read music. Until recently ballet choreography wasn't recorded in notated form. It was handed down by choreographers, ballet masters and mistresses who had danced many roles themselves, and then handed on their encyclopaedic and practical knowledge to the next generation. Video footage from previous performances is very useful, and these days is used a lot, but it has the same pitfalls as a singer learning an opera from a sound recording. Mistakes happen in live performance, and that's how mistakes accidentally end up becoming 'tradition'.

Since the mid-twentieth century, forms of notation have been used to record choreography, to keep track as the choreographer creates a new work, or to recreate older productions. The most famous form is Benesh Movement Notation. It shares similarities with musical notation. It is written on a five-line stave, and sometimes has bar lines and tempo markings that correspond exactly with the music. As in an orchestral score, in large ensembles where different groups of dancers are performing simultaneously, the staves are linked together vertically. Just as higher notes appear on the upper lines of a musical stave, shapes and lines on the upper lines of a BMN score represent gestures of the upper body. The difference is that composers and everyone performing Western classical music use the same notation. Notating and reading BMN, on the other hand, is a specialism that only a few people working in ballet possess. Traditionally a composer sits at a desk, piano or more recently an electric keyboard linked to a computer and writes down the sounds in their head. A choreographer works more like a stage director. They will do much preparation in advance of the first rehearsal but create the choreography with live beings – the dancers. Some of today's composers and Baroque composers might have had a looser creative process and allow more improvisation from musicians themselves, but essentially musicians are reading and reproducing what has already been written down.

Rehearsals

The rehearsal process is not dissimilar to opera. There is a lengthy rehearsal period in the studio, followed by stage-and-piano/technical rehearsals. The conductor will have rehearsed the orchestra separately and the stage-and-orchestra rehearsals are the final piece of the jigsaw.

The studio rehearsals might be stretched out over a longer period, while other ballets are being rehearsed simultaneously. Ballet companies usually comprise full-time dancers

– *corps de ballet* and soloists. It's similar to the model many European opera houses employ – a full-time chorus and soloists. Guest soloists are rare. Also, there's a simple but brutal hierarchy and a meritocracy in ballet, where everyone starts in the *corps de ballet* and the best get fast-tracked to become soloists and principal dancers. A dancer's career is short and intense, and most retire by forty, some transferring to teaching, administrative or artistic leadership roles within the company or completely retraining and starting a new career.

The role of a conductor in the studio is very different from their role in an opera house as they are not as integral to the creative process. There is no need for purely musical rehearsals at the start and the conductor does not lead the rehearsal as the choreography is created. They are not exactly relegated to a lower status but the position is off-putting for many conductors, who struggle with not being in charge. A choreographer will have found a favourite recording, and will sometimes believe that is the only way the music can go. There's no doubt this can be a frustrating experience, and heated discussions can arise. It can be hard for a conductor to stand their ground in the climate of a ballet company.

BARRY WORDSWORTH: I put this down to the fact that a conductor is always employed by an ex-dancer. So, if there's any stress, or difficulty, their instinct is to side with the choreographer or the producer of the ballet. That's something you must try to overcome by winning their trust. You can't always be the person who says, 'Yes.' I will say, 'No, because I can't get the orchestra to play like that. It will ruin our discipline.' That's a challenge to the way choreographers work, and that's why there are conductors who just don't want to be bothered with it. I understand and respect that.

I've always said that ballet conducting is something that you should love to do, but never do a hundred per cent. Always get away from it, give yourself a break. But you must get used to being told how a piece of music is supposed to go by people who don't read a note of music, and that can be quite irksome at times.

Ballet Pianists

Ballet pianists come prepared and play for all the rehearsals. It's all about the choreographer (in a new work), or the ballet masters/mistresses teaching the steps. The conductor should be there as much as possible in these rehearsals, but dipping in and out, and usually conducting the pianist.

BARRY WORDSWORTH: I believe the conductor of a ballet needs to be present for a significant part of this lengthy rehearsal process. We need to be in from the start – not necessarily every day. It can happen that some days you'll go to the studio and come away and think, 'Well, there was no point my being there.' But you can't prophesy. You dip in from the start, and then your dipping in becomes more frequent as you come closer to the performance.

The conductor can learn much from the pianist, and they will know the tempi the dancers have got used to. They will have been listening very carefully to what's going on in the studio, so that when the choreographer is explaining something and then asks for the music to start again, they will know exactly at what point. This can be a challenge when none of the ballet staff can read music. The music staff and conductor will need to understand ballet terms, which are mostly in French or a combination of French and English. The pianist's score will be littered with markings, so that when they say, 'Go from 8 into the second manège, please!', they can start without any fuss. It's good for the conductor to write at least some of these cues into their score.

There are some companies (not the main UK ones) that have dispensed with their pianists, usually for financial reasons, and work solely or partially to recordings. In cases when much of the music is electronic, then of course that is necessary, but it is not a good direction to be heading in for most repertoire.

Ballet Class

Ballet pianists are as invaluable as their opera counterpart – the répétiteur – but their skillset is different. They play for ballet class every day. This is an essential part of a dancer's life. Led by a ballet teacher, every professional company will start with one and three-quarter hours warming up together before they begin rehearsing. The pianist will play for this, improvising music in different styles, tempi and time signatures to suit their movements. The teacher leads the dancers as they warm their bodies from standing at the barre into their most active steps as they fly across the floor.

BARRY WORDSWORTH: As soon as I started working in ballet, I immediately admired the hard work that dancers do. Every morning, starting at 10 a.m., and finishing at 10 p.m., sometimes without a break at all. I remember thinking, 'If I'd practised the harpsichord that much . . .' I sometimes played for ballet class and it was quite fun. I was not as good as the ballet pianists, because I'm not a very good jazz pianist. In the middle of class on a Friday when everyone is tired, it really helps if the pianist jazzes it up a bit.

In order to help me understand singing technique, I took singing lessons, and even that was scratching the surface because I would never get close to producing the sound my professional singer colleagues could make. When I first started conducting ballet, I needed to do the same thing, but it would have to be purely from an observational position. Dancers seem to be an entirely different specimen of human form from the conductor, and this is the major challenge for the ballet conductor. The sensation of leaping across the stage can only be imagined by most of us. The best way of sensing this tempo is by watching. I observed many ballet classes, and like Barry was bowled over by their discipline. The studios are always overheated to prevent dancers' muscles from getting cold. From my sedentary position in the corner, I confess it didn't help me feel great about any weight as I approached my forties, and lethargy and sleepiness would overwhelm me.

For some reason I've never fathomed, classical musicians are usually blessed with very limited dancing abilities. I think much of this has to do with the rigid way we have been taught, and the focus on the aural. Singers are usually better at this, and very often have to dance, but the rest of us are mostly just hopeless and embarrassed by it. All musicians can sing in tune, yet that other fundamental form of human musical expression has been squeezed out of us somewhere along the way. It is there somewhere, and some brilliant performers have embraced this in recent years – the Scottish Ensemble's choreographed *Goldberg Variations*, for example – but this is still rare. Many conductors seem to have the two-left-feet gene, though now that there are more women in the profession, this seems to be changing a little. There is, however, one notable exception.

An Exception

Maria Seletskaja was a soloist at the Estonian National Ballet, the Royal Flanders Ballet, the Berlin State Opera Ballet and the Zurich Opera Ballet. Before she retired as a dancer, she began retraining as a conductor and in 2020 she was appointed Conductor-in-Residence at the National Ballet of Canada. This extraordinary achievement wasn't a sudden switch in career, and is down to her talent, extraordinary discipline, and passion for music. Music was at the heart of her life even before she began dancing, and early on in her career a seed was sown.

MARIA SELETSKAJA: It was my first season at Estonian National Ballet. I was nineteen and managed to injure myself in the first two weeks. I was miserable. Then the *Nutcracker* season started, and I heard the orchestra rehearsing. Talking to a violinist afterwards, I said, 'I would give two years of my life to stand in front of an orchestra and just wave my hands to the music of Tchaikovsky. I know you can play it by yourself, but I would love to experience how it feels.' Instead of laughing, he said, 'We all know that you are practising the piano every day until midnight. Why don't you become a ballet conductor?'

There have been people who would appear for longer or shorter periods in my life, creating some sort of support for me, because I had no idea in which direction to go. No one had become a conductor before. I could have said, 'I want to land on the moon without a space suit.' Yet there was always someone who would give me perfectly tailored advice for that moment. These conductors never laughed as I came rushing up to them in my tutu after a performance.

Aside from obvious natural talent, passion, drive and discipline, Maria has another key factor working in her favour. She was born in the Soviet Union.

In the Soviet system, every child had amazing opportunities to study whatever (be it sports, dance, music) at an extremely high level, and thankfully it is still so in Estonia.

And unlike most Western specialist ballet schools, her music studies continued throughout.

If you were accepted into ballet school, it meant you had ballet training, the regular school curriculum and an obligatory five years of piano, history of music, music analysis and solfège (ear training). They believed it contributed strongly to your understanding and developing craftsmanship qualities as an artist. When you dance, you need to know what you are dancing to.

Maria never stopped studying piano, and her teacher would cry in her lesson, claiming she could have a career as a concert pianist.

Slowly the seed from that conversation back in Tallinn began to sprout. Maria started looking at scores of the music she was dancing to, causing quite a stir in the orchestra when she addressed a conductor from the stage in their language. 'Please could we take it from three bars after the *fortissimo,* when the brass enter?' There was a slow raising of heads from the pit, as the players peered meerkat-like up at the stage.

Alongside her full-time job as a dancer, she took a correspondence course in advanced studies in music theory at Berklee College of Music, private conducting lessons with resident conductors, and short conducting courses. The powers that be in these institutions began to recognise her seriousness and talent, and assisting opportunities started to appear. By the time she performed for the last time as a dancer, she had already conducted performances. Though used to being in the spotlight, nothing prepared her for the shock of her conducting debut.

At Stuttgart Ballet I was assisting on *La Fille mal gardée*, and I wasn't supposed to conduct any shows, but I did a lot of piano run-throughs and the ballet director decided to give me a chance. I was terrified, but I knew I had to say yes. Alone in a room, I ran the whole ballet twice a day for three weeks until I could conduct the whole thing by heart. As I dreamed of becoming a conductor, I had often imagined the moment of walking to the podium – the doors of the pit opening flamboyantly, me sweeping in and bowing to two thousand people wildly applauding. The reality was completely different. I was still dancing at the time and was very thin. I could see the orchestra looking at me thinking, 'Little girl! Who are you? We can play it without you.' I felt like Mr Bean with this beam of light shining on me. For sure the first ten minutes their heads were down, and they mostly ignored me. Their job is to play together, and they didn't believe I would help with that. But because I was conducting from memory, I could look at players and really make eye contact. By the end of the first tableau, we were starting to make music together.

When we spoke in early 2021, she was back in Estonia studying at the Academy for a master's in conducting alongside piano and violin lessons. And she is in good hands with teachers from both the St Petersburg and Moscow conducting schools.

> I felt I needed to be studying at this level, so I can finally erase the last doubts I had that I am not enough of a musician, that I am just a self-proclaimed conductor. If I was criticised as a dancer, I would always work hard to correct it, but I would still be terribly upset and take it personally. It's different with conducting. I feel very happy to have a strict teacher. He says 'OK, I know that you can conduct, but I won't get off your neck until you do it better, because I know you are disciplined enough and won't give up.'

As Maria quickly catches up on the technical side of the job, she has an obvious advantage over the rest of us. Yet that comes with responsibility and pressure.

> I feel that dancers require nothing but a perfect tempo from me. You know the famous joke that for dancers there are only two tempi – too slow or too fast. And dancers know they have to eat what is being served up by the conductor. But when I'm conducting, I feel a slight off tempo is perceived very strongly by them. They judge me more harshly.

In Good Hands

The conductor will need to use their eyes like ears, while still using their normal conducting ears. Ballet staff will hear music with their eyes, and dancers will hear it with their whole body, but not necessarily their ears. The music can be played at precisely the same tempo as before, but because the dancers are struggling with something, it might sound too fast or too slow to the person teaching the steps. It's good for a conductor to be consistent in rehearsals and performances, sticking to the same tempo, while understanding that flexibility is needed. Early on in rehearsals, when dancers are learning steps or even early in a run of performances, the tempo might be fractionally slower. We are talking here about such tiny margins – fifty-nine beats to a second instead of sixty, but it can be enough to make the difference.

> The National Ballet of Canada accepts me fully as part
> of their family. However, they expect me to read their
> current condition, both emotionally and physically,
> because this has an impact on the way dancers move. If a
> dancer is tired, every tempo feels too fast and if they are
> on high adrenalin, every tempo feels too slow. So, you
> need to understand not only what's happening, but also
> to choose and clearly indicate to the orchestra the correct
> tempo.

That is why the Estonian-American conductor and teacher Paavo Järvi says that every conductor needs to experience conducting ballet. He claims that you cannot possess the technique required to be completely in control of an orchestra unless you have conducted ballet.

Repertoire

There is some tremendous repertoire for the ballet conductor. Ballet works by Tchaikovsky, Prokofiev and Stravinsky are generally acknowledged to include some of the greatest music in the orchestral repertoire, often also enjoying a life in the concert hall. There are many fine composers today and particularly in the twentieth century who have been commissioned to write ballet scores. A particularly rewarding experience was *New Works*, an event I conducted at the Royal Opera House's Linbury Theatre. It was a showcase for upcoming choreographers from The Royal Ballet, including Jonathan Watkins, who commissioned a work by the composer Graham Fitkin. It was a highlight for me, and an occasion when the experience was definitely a three-way collaboration: choreographer, composer, conductor.

There's a growing popularity from the last century onwards of choreographers turning to the standard orchestral repertoire for their inspiration. On a tour with Birmingham Royal Ballet, I conducted Elgar's *Enigma Variations* and Tchaikovsky's *Serenade for Strings* in the same programme. What a treat! And, unlike with a programme for a symphonic concert, there were many performances. Barry Wordsworth claims he has probably conducted Mahler's *Das Lied von der Erde* more times than Bernard Haitink.

It can't be denied that some of the classical repertoire, a visual feast though it may be, is not the greatest music. Like Tchaikovsky, the Viennese composer Ludwig Minkus, working mostly in Russia, collaborated with Petipa and provided the scores for some of the most famous works in classical ballet. His ballet *Don Quixote* is still very much part of the staple diet of companies today. The role of the music is to serve the visuals and it doesn't stand up particularly well on its own.

> BARRY WORDSWORTH: I promised myself on my fortieth birthday that I would never conduct Minkus again. I haven't kept that promise, but I am not a great Minkus fan, I have to say.

Perhaps that was my problem with *La Fille mal gardée* all those years ago. This is the music I must have heard, and the version most performed during these past sixty years. It was skilfully created by the conductor and composer John Lanchbery, who took music from two earlier versions by Ferdinand Hérold and Peter Hertel and added his own pastiche compositions. There's no doubting the brilliance of this ballet and that the music and dance are a perfect fit, but for a child with a natural musical ear, perhaps it just wasn't enough to draw me in. The job of a conductor is more as a craftsman than as an artist in this work. There's some satisfaction in doing that well, but it has its limitations.

Yet some ballet music is misunderstood, and I again would draw the analogy with opera. Not all musicians love or

understand operas of the Italian nineteenth-century bel canto era. Only when the text, drama and story are understood
and the beautiful line of the melody is produced does the
simple accompaniment make sense. Then it comes alive. Bellini's *Norma* was written just ten years before Adolphe Adam's
Giselle and they are not dissimilar. The music of the former
serves beautiful singing and the latter beautiful dancing.

A Bridge between Two Worlds

The conductor's role is to inspire the orchestra, to transcend
the technical challenges. It's very tempting to play it safe and
not take care over the sound and the phrasing, if you are
constantly being told the tempo is too fast or too slow.

BARRY WORDSWORTH: It is very easy for the orchestra
to turn off. I can remember meeting friends from the
orchestra walking down from Angel tube station to Sadler's
Wells, when opera was also performed there. I'd ask,
'What are you playing tonight?' and they'd say, 'Oh, it's
La traviata, and we've got this amazing Violetta, and this
conductor, but the Alfredo has gone off sick, someone else
has come in.' They were buzzing with the excitement of
it. On another night it was 'Oh, er . . . just some ballet.'
And I thought, 'This is going to be the one thing I will try
to do. I will try to make their ballet nights as satisfying as
their opera nights.' It's a lovely challenge.

I think it's terribly important that everybody has

a chance to find out what it's like to have a better understanding of this musical world and of what it means to be a ballet musician. The ROH had a lovely partnership with a professional training orchestra, Southbank Sinfonia, where we would do a mixed weekend of opera and ballet excerpts. Members of the Royal Opera House Orchestra would sit side by side with these young instrumentalists, coaching them. For the ballet excerpts I used to ask for the whole orchestra to sit in the stalls as our ballet pianist played for the dancers. Members of the ROH Orchestra would say afterwards, 'Barry, we should all do this. Now I understand why you conduct the way you do, why we have to slow down there – to allow them to get into the far corner of the stage.' It was a revelation and was motivating.

There is a similar problem with opera, when orchestras are impatient with singers who seemingly have a poor sense of rhythm. I say to them, 'Have you actually seen what they are doing at that moment?' It would be wonderful if every orchestral player would attend some stage-and-piano re-hearsals, but time is money, and sadly no company in the world has those resources. I try to encourage students playing in college opera productions at least to attend a piano dress rehearsal if they can. It makes a difference.

Maria sees her responsibility from the other side:

I present myself as a bridge between two worlds. I am an ice-breaker. It's funny because there are so many dancers who dream about becoming musicians, especially conductors, but they never dared. They are afraid to approach musicians. Instrumentalists are seen as demigods and conductors as gods.

Maria is already acting as a mentor to some talented musicians who happen to be dancers:

I always knew that dancing was not my end destination. As a graduate of the Vaganova Ballet Academy in St Petersburg I should have felt that ballet is everything; in a way it was, otherwise I would not have made it. And, yes, I have made a career, not a stellar career, but a career at a high level. I cannot say I was unhappy, but there was some sort of uncertainty inside. I always cared what other people thought about me. I always felt I wasn't good enough. In the end it took its toll on me because the nervous system starts giving up after decades of beating yourself up.

For me conducting is not a profession, but a passion, a calling. This I will do until I drop dead. I know I have galaxies to learn, but it doesn't bother me.

I'm glad to have learned some of these skills, and to be able to keep my hand in with occasional engagements, but I am full of admiration for those who have made it their specialism. I have no doubt that these experiences made me a better conductor and have helped me better understand that relationship between stage and pit.

9: New Music

Are You a Composer?

It's amazing how often people outside my working world accidently call me a composer. That's when the hand-waving conducting mime comes in handy. It always surprises and sometimes irritates me, but it really shouldn't. It's not just because both words begin and end with the same letters, nor that they have the same stress on the second of three syllables. There has always been a strong link and a crossover in skills, so it's quite a natural assumption.

I have never had any desire to compose, and while I wasn't discouraged at school, I just missed out on it being part of the music curriculum. I was the last year of O levels, and I am very glad about that. We studied the harmonic and compositional structures of a wide variety of works, and that gave me a terrific foundation. But the syllabus didn't include original composition, which was compulsory a year later for those taking GCSE music. Perhaps being forced to write something would have lit a fire. As part of my musical education through to degree level, I learned to write pastiche music of the sixteenth to nineteenth centuries and this was the best way of studying harmonic and compositional styles from the inside out, but it never made me curious to create my own sound world. In my twenties I was growing to love contemporary music and was friends with some upcoming composers. Long and fascinating conversations with them made me totally in awe of their brains, ears and imaginations, and their passion to keep creating new music. I figured there was enough music being written by people who needed to give birth to their creations. There seemed little point in my writing something that didn't want to be written. I'd rather help with realising it once the hardest bit is done. It's always a privilege to be involved in this type of collaboration.

Premieres

In the depths of winter and the gloom of February 2021 I took an empty train up to Glasgow to conduct the Royal Scottish National Orchestra in a recording of a new work by Jonathan Dove – *Gaspard's Foxtrot*. As with its companion piece, Prokofiev's *Peter and the Wolf*, this story was written by Zeb Soanes specifically to be set to music. The RSNO pulled out all the stops, creating beautiful animation from James Mayhew's illustrations, and making it free to all Scottish primary schools. Zeb recorded his narration in another room, and I conducted a socially distanced orchestra. Normally the composer would be present at the recording, especially if the piece has never been performed before, and I love this interaction, but we made it work with Jonathan in his London studio wired up to video, audio, Zoom and WhatsApp.

Classical musicians spend much of their lives deciphering pages of music written by dead people. Despite the wonderfully varied interpretations we inevitably give, our aim is to be as faithful to the composer's intentions as possible. Valuable research into historical performance practice and references to original manuscripts has allowed us to be remarkably accurate. Yet we sometimes tie ourselves in knots worrying over a little detail that isn't quite working and musing over a composer's decision on certain things. In our recording session, on the rare occasion where something didn't quite work, Jonathan's voice sounded from the speaker by my podium: 'Ah, yes, change that — to this —.'

That same year, in the height of summer, I was back conducting *Gaspard's Foxtrot* again with the Philharmonia Orchestra in Malvern as part of the Three Choirs Festival. This time with a live audience of children and parents (and Jonathan), so it was the world premiere. We also performed *Peter and the Wolf* in that concert, and I spoke to the audience between pieces – seeing if they could recognise the different instruments. Gaspard was represented by a bassoon, which one child (admittedly a very young child) thought was a guitar. 'Well, they are both made of wood,' I said encouragingly. Another character in the story is represented by the harp, or the 'heart' as one child rather touchingly called it.

A few months later I couldn't have been tackling more contrasting subject matter in a workshop for a new opera by the composer Conor Mitchell based on rape and sexual harassment trials – power and the abuse of power. It is an unusual privilege for a conductor to be involved so early on, but that is the way of the innovative Belfast Ensemble.

Conor cleverly and wisely involves representatives from the whole company, so they are invested from the start.

Specialists

These days most conductors expect to conduct new music on a regular basis, and I love this. Concert programmes, even at the more traditional end, tend to include a decent amount of music by living composers. However, just as some focus on ballet or opera, others get a reputation for specialising in contemporary repertoire, and many of those are also composers themselves. One such person is Richard Baker.

RICHARD BAKER: I remember my first encounter [as a young chorister at Lichfield Cathedral] with what you might call contemporary music – Britten, Stravinsky and so on. I couldn't really articulate what it was doing to me, but I just knew this was what I wanted. So, I started writing some terrible music from the age of about nine.

By the time he went to Oxford University, champing at the bit to perform all things contemporary, he quickly formed his own contemporary music ensemble – the wittily named Oxford Elastic Band. He went on to study composition with Louis Andriessen in The Hague.

I was very young compared with many of the students and it was quite a shock going from the free-for-all

Oxbridge culture to a very rigid European conservatoire environment. I wanted to continue performing new music but was told, 'Don't be silly! Only people on the conducting course can do that.' There was a more professional attitude to music-making, and it felt that my wings had been clipped slightly. However, the composition teaching was incredible, and the richly funded music scene meant I could go to world-class performances every night incredibly cheaply.

His focus was on composition though he continued having conducting lessons. The desire simply to make new music happen, rather than calling himself a conductor, was what attracted him.

In 2004 a Gerald Barry portrait concert was programmed at the Aldeburgh Festival, and it included a piece called *Bob*. It's wonderful, but incredibly difficult – fifteen minutes, very fast, with every bar in a different metre. When they realised about two months before that it needed a conductor, the composer John Woolrich suggested me. At the time I was nursing my father who was in the final stages of a terminal illness. It was a kind of displacement activity – an excuse to study and focus on something that wasn't the horror going on next door. I have never been more prepared for anything in my entire life. It went well. The composer and conductor Oliver Knussen was in the audience and said, 'Were you scared of *Bob*? It scares the bejesus out of me.' If I'd known then how terrifying that piece was, there's no way I would have conducted it. When I think about it now, it was a completely ridiculous thing for me to have done.

When I am learning a score written in the twentieth century, I always try to seek out recordings by composers themselves. Surely their performances will be the gold standard? It's always an interesting listen, but it's a huge challenge to do both.

RICHARD BAKER: I find it very stressful to conduct my own premieres. Conducting any new piece is challenging because the players don't know the music, they don't know the language, and the conductor must create a shape and interpretation where everything is working. But as the composer you have the added anxiety of hearing it for the first time and feeling you might have miscalculated certain moments. So, you have all the self-consciousness one normally has as a conductor, plus the self-consciousness of being the composer. Latterly I have asked others to conduct my premieres. I have a big orchestral piece coming up, and I'm glad I'm not conducting that. I look at the score and think, 'If this came through the post for me to conduct, I would be absolutely terrified.'

Preparation

Preparing a new score has its own challenges, but huge

advantages too, not least because you can pick up the phone or have a Zoom meeting, or even an in-person coffee with the composer. I love having the composer in the room for the rehearsals too, although sometimes it's better for them not to be around for the very first run-through. When the players are still figuring out how to play it, there can be an unnecessary level of stress that dissipates later in the process.

ANTONIO PAPPANO: Learning a complex contemporary work can be torture at the start, but in a way it is easier to organise because at first it is just a maths problem, and that can be a fun part of the journey. In an opera using text to find the direction, the bass lines, the implied harmony, what is decorative, and what is essential, all those things can be applied, just as in more standard repertoire.

MARIN ALSOP: Preparing a completely new score is like trying to learn a new language very quickly – finding the commonalities, because every composer has their own vocabulary. I enjoy it because there's nothing prescribed about it, so I can bring more to it. I don't have to battle through many centuries of tradition to get to the essence of what the piece is. I think I've gotten much faster at preparing a new piece. I know how to take it apart, whereas with standard repertoire, where you're trying to make a statement and really develop it, that takes me much longer now than it used to.

Most of the new works I have conducted are at the more traditional end of the scale, and in terms of learning the scores, I can rely on playing them at the piano and using my inner ear – hearing it in my head – though it's far harder than in Classical and Romantic repertoire. There's a freedom in not listening to recordings, but synthesised mock-ups are sometimes useful, especially in very complex works. This technology has improved in recent years, but like any text-to-audio software, it has its limitations and artificiality.

Synchronisation

The click track is used to synchronise music with something visual on stage or screen that needs a precise timing, or to synchronise two recordings that have been made separately but need to be patched together. The conductor and some players (very often the percussion section) have an earpiece relaying a beat. The first time I had to work with this was in a tap-dance number for a Christmas show. The floor was too soft for the tap shoe sound to be heard over the orchestra, so it was pre-recorded on a harder floor. Because we were always performing to the same tempo, the dancers' feet could land on the floor exactly at the same time as the audience heard the tap-shoe sound. I had to start the click track with a foot pedal, which on most occasions I did, but for one performance my foot accidently pressed it on and off, and then on again. The audience that evening was treated to a confusing visual/audio experience.

RICHARD BAKER: Recently I have conducted some operas
with a click track. Philip Venables's *4.48 Psychosis* (an
adaption of Sarah Kane's play) was dependent on perfect
synchronisation with the stage. It was so effective, though it
was a very odd experience – like you're being plugged into a
machine rather than driving it. You're at the mercy of a stage
manager, calling a cue to a sound operator at the back of
the stage who then presses a space bar. In live performances
there's an adrenalin in players. In exciting music, they might
want to get slightly faster, but can't because of the click.
Learning just to trust that it will work is important.

Film and Media

Musicians working in recording sessions, particularly in
soundtracks for films, are very comfortable with synchronisation, and for Eímear Noone the world is familiar and
natural to her:

Synchronisation is a relatively new art form, particularly
as we begin to work with orchestras in real time. It could
be a film or holograms, and what's going to happen soon
will be synchronising to AR, which adds another layer
of complexity and an avenue for creativity. When the
orchestra and technology meet, depending on whose brains
are at work, it can be fabulous, or it can be a train wreck.
It's like an opera. You want to have the very best creative
brains when these resources are put together.

Eímear is the first woman to conduct at the Oscars and her career is mostly focused on another area of composition and conducting – film and gaming music. Her background is founded in classical music, and she studied composition and flute at Trinity College Dublin.

Throughout my life there have been angels who have helped me. When I was about fifteen, I took part in a composition workshop with Colin Mawby and the National Chamber Choir of Ireland. I had the music in my head, but no idea how to write it down, but despite that, Colin seemed to see something there behind the messiness. At the end of the workshop he said, 'Go home and tidy up your handwriting, and we will perform your piece for RTÉ at Dublin Castle!' A few years later I received a letter from the University of California at Los Angeles inviting me to take part in their 'Composition for Film' course. I was surprised because I hadn't applied, and I discovered that Colin had entered me. He was one of my angels.

My fascination has always been the visceral reaction to music. The job of a film and gaming composer is to create an environment, to tell a story, and to set up or deliberately solicit an emotion from an audience. When you've learned the harmonic language, and the style of orchestration, it's then a question of taking it from a craft to an art.

The one area of conducting I am yet to venture into is

film, and Eímear brings this to life as she describes her very
specialised job:

> In the recording studio, we're always thinking about how
> the music will be used by the rest of the team. The dub
> stage is where we artificially create the audio environment
> of cinema. We mix the music for the score, and the sound
> designers create the explosions, walking noises and the
> Foley. These sounds are mixed, and then you have the
> dialogue editors and mixers making sure they all work
> together. Then there's foreground and background. It is
> a many-layered process.
>
> For financial reasons, a recording session is like a
> military campaign. We normally record about 6 to 8
> minutes of music in a 50-minute hour. The 10-minute
> break is so important. In those 50 minutes you get all the
> juice, and if you go over an hour, you end up discarding
> more. In preparation for a recording, I will work out
> how long the sections can be, where the tempo changes
> seamlessly and I can keep going, and where we will likely
> need to restart. This saves time and money, and the
> orchestra appreciates that. There's a lot of stress, politics
> and expectations going on in a studio and the stress
> increases with the budget. However, the higher the budget,
> the more experienced the team and the easier it is to work
> because everyone knows what they're doing.
>
> There are different methods of synchronisation, and it
> has to do with what role the music is playing – whether

it needs to be pinpoint accurate. Some require audio cues like a click track, and others need visual cues on the screen, which we call 'punches' and 'streamers'. This comes from the early days of Hollywood when they had a big clock in front of the score. The conductor looks at a screen with a green line going across (the streamer) until it reaches a flash (the punch). In the past this was drawn on the actual tape with a marker pen and the punches were made by a hole punch. These days it's digital. It's a kind of visual metronome.

Live synchronisation can take many weird and wonderful forms. I got the shock of my life when an entire row of fountains went off on one of my downbeats in a concert in China. Then there was the launch of the twenty-fifth anniversary of the huge Nintendo title *The Legend of Zelda*. In downtown LA, I was in the basement of Nokia Live with some of my favourite session players, crammed onto a caged-in stage. We were given a cue to start playing, and suddenly there was a motor sound beneath us. We started moving up through the floor and appeared to an audience of eight thousand screaming fans.

Female Composers

It's interesting though a little disappointing that when I am asked to conduct premieres it's nearly always music by male composers. The visibility of female composers is improving and there are many more women enjoying successful careers today with fabulous young composers coming through, but my experience would suggest we are not quite there yet.

In 2019 Decca released an album I conducted of previously unrecorded music by women involved in the British Suffrage movement. Naturally it included Ethel Smyth's *March of the Women*, which she famously conducted with a toothbrush from her prison window. There were other call-to-arms works by barely known composers with titles including *Fighting On*, *Give Me My Freedom*, and *Our Hard Case*. Quite extraordinarily this was the first ever commercial recording to be made with an entirely female team – composers, arrangers, musicians, singers, speakers, producer and sound engineer. Also on the album was an arrangement by the producer Juliette Pochin of Katherine Eggar's beautifully haunting *Idyll*. Almost exactly a hundred years between the founding of the Society of Women Musicians and my Women Conductors programme, I feel a great kinship with its co-founder Katherine Eggar, and was proud to help bring her music to life again.

The sessions, which took less than a day, were great fun, fast and efficient. I couldn't resist bringing my toothbrush, though I decided to stick to the baton. The songs and marches were to a click track, so the choir could be added later with Ellie Slorach conducting. There was an amusing moment when I asked for the orchestra to go from bar 69. In some British orchestras there has been a tradition that mention of this bar number (by female or male conductors) be accompanied by a little cheer and a foot shuffle. You might call it 'British humour', and it is I think quite harmless levity, with no intention of causing offence, though in recent years I've noticed it happens less. I paused to allow for that moment to pass, but there was silence. It's certainly not only men who make these noises usually, but clearly the absence of them made the orchestra feel it unnecessary to point out the rude number. This made us all laugh.

Over the centuries, composers have written beautiful pieces of music that allow instrumentalists to focus on technique. No one, as far as I know, has written something specifically for conductors to practise their craft. There are of course works (certain symphonies and overtures) that lend themselves to teaching, and Musin certainly had his favourites. Something I was all too aware of with the WoCo workshops was how few works we were using by female composers. In 2018 my colleagues at the Royal Philharmonic Society and I took a day trip to the Red House in Aldeburgh – the home of Benjamin Britten. There's a huge archive there, including works not only by Britten, but other composers associated with him, including Imogen Holst. I normally include music by her father Gustav, and we found the manuscript of a little piece she wrote for strings when she was twenty-one, which Colin Matthews kindly edited, and which we now use regularly in our workshops. In August 2022 this received its world premiere at the Dartington Festival – ninety-five years late.

The RPS went one step further and with the Ralph Vaughan Williams Trust commissioned Cecilia McDowall to write a work to be recorded by the London Mozart

Players. *Off the Ground* enjoys its own life and is not simply to be used as a teaching tool. By the time I conducted it in a concert at Kings Place with the Southbank Sinfonia in September 2021, it had already received two live performances. I was able to chat to Cecilia before she wrote it about the things that I am looking for in a teaching piece. It's full of challenges with changes in tempi, character and time signatures – a marvellously energetic work, perfect for some of our conducting workshops.

10: Reaching Out

A Musician for Life

We tend to shy away from the word 'amateur', seeing it as a somewhat patronising term meaning sloppy, casual and uncaring, though well-meaning and enthusiastic. But shouldn't all musicians be amateurs? It comes from the French word meaning 'lover'. Are we not all lovers of music – professional and non-professional, performers and listeners? I would hope so.

What happens to all these talented hard-working children who are lucky enough to be born in the right time, place or circumstances to have music as an essential part of their life? There is a complex multifaceted world out there.

Many go on to university and music college and choose to work in this huge industry, as performers, composers, teachers, administrators, producers, technicians, or develop a portfolio career combining many of the above. Many more, who don't go on to work in music, take their childhood passion right through their lives.

There are thousands of non-professional music ensembles in the UK and the amateur music-making tradition is one of the richest. Some of these groups are well over a hundred years old and most were founded by and for the community. Nor was this intended just for the middle classes. In the

nineteenth and twentieth centuries almost every coal mine
in the country had its own brass band, and this tradition has
outlived the mines themselves.

> SIAN EDWARDS: One of the greatest honours was when I
> was invited to conduct the Williams Fairey Engineering
> Brass Band in Stockport. They had a corrugated-iron pre-
> war band room on the factory premises which only just
> fitted the band. It was almost as if the walls were pulsating
> as the band made this beautiful sound.

There is something for everyone out there, from former
National Youth Orchestra players who chose other career
paths but still want to perform at a high level, to the person
who starts or returns to an instrument much later in life.
The repertoire is varied too, from standard classical works
to jazz and big band, from chamber choirs focusing on
Renaissance music to the 'Can't Sing' community choirs.
They all seek that joy of making music together and, as
with most evening clubs, a pint in the pub afterwards is just
as important for many.

All these orchestras and ensembles need a conductor, and
this provides so many opportunities for conductors at all
levels.

Post-Russia, my first position where I was able to cut
my teeth with an orchestra was in Sweden. Not long after I
moved there and was working at Gothenburg Opera, I was
appointed artistic director of the Borås Symphony Orchestra

and held the position for three years. Borås is an industrial town, famous for its textile industry, not far from Gothenburg. The orchestra was founded in 1912 by a group of local musicians and for many decades was called Borås orkesterföreningen – the Borås Community Orchestra. As with its UK counterparts, community is at its heart, but by the time I was there they had created an interesting semi-professional model. Everyone was paid, but on a sliding scale. There were some professional musicians at union pay rates, music students at a lower rate, and amateurs were paid expenses only. They all attended the same number of rehearsals. It seemed to work, with a high commitment level for rehearsals, and a condensed rehearsal period (rather than weekly) helped with that. The concert hall, Åhaga, was a converted train factory – a huge versatile space, used for community and conference events and complete with a real steam train. With the support of professionals and music students, we could tackle challenging repertoire and engaged some excellent soloists for concertos and arias, and sometimes used local choirs. Over those three years I started to build up repertoire and the all-important podium experience.

I have had a few guest engagements with amateur orchestras since then and have been involved in training youth orchestras, which I love. I am glad this work came later in my career. There's a big responsibility in training the next generation, and I certainly benefited from a little more maturity and experience. It is different and harder work because the conductor must fix more things – for example, the approach to solving intonation problems. Just as with a professional orchestra, intonation can improve as the players become more familiar with the music. But the skills involved, the highly developed listening and technical mastery of the instrument, comes out of years of training. The youth orchestra conductor is partly responsible for that training, along with teaching good ensemble and how to watch a conductor.

Conducting an amateur or youth orchestra can be a good starting point for an upcoming conductor, but therein lies the danger of considering it to be easier work. It requires a level of maturity and personal as well as musical insight that can't be learned overnight. As music director of the Blackpool Symphony Orchestra, Preston Opera, Lytham St Anne's Choral Society, former music director of the Lancashire Youth Symphony Orchestra, and as the recently appointed music director of the Royal Northern Sinfonia's youth orchestra, Helen Harrison is representative of a group of highly skilled conductors who enjoy full-time conducting careers mostly working with non-professional orchestras:

> It's a big responsibility. An established professional
> orchestra is like a river that's flowing, and the conductor
> can move the eddies around, but you can't dam it up and
> make it go backwards. You can with an amateur orchestra.
> We talk about music being something that connects
> people, and it's important that there is music of the very
> highest professional standards, but the quality of music-
> making needs to be valued across the patch. If we don't

value the music-making of our local amateur orchestras,
then how can we expect the highest quality to be valued
in society? But this is the challenge. In the amateur music
world, there are highly successful people in their own
fields, and this is how they choose to spend their spare
time, often paying for the privilege. As the professional
musician in the group, I still want the music to be the
best it can possibly be. The dynamic with a professional
orchestra is different because they must deliver whether
they are in the mood or not. I am mindful that amateur
ensembles are run by volunteers, who could just vote with
their feet and leave.

Helen has a similar musical background and education
to many of the most lauded conductors in this country. She
went to Cambridge to read Music, and she flourished. Her
college, Corpus Christi, had a thriving musical life, and she
conducted a lot, as well as playing in ensembles. How she
found time for this I don't know, but she was also captain of
the college football team and president of the Junior Common Room.

Music was my focus, but most of my social life was
college-based, and I knew there were many things I
could do with my life other than music. I had friends
from youth orchestra who were at music college and not
particularly happy. I didn't know about all the different
careers you could have in music. After the last concert I

conducted in Cambridge someone asked if I was going
to do a master's in conducting at music college. I didn't
even know that was an option. I had played in Cambridge
University Chamber Orchestra, where both Sian Edwards
and Jane Glover were guest conductors at the time, but I
just hadn't made the connection.

Helen moved to Japan for a year, where she taught English.
Music was still important, and she joined an orchestra there.

One day a teacher who worked in my school left me a
message on my desk: 'Please meet me here tomorrow and
we play Bach Double Violin Concerto.' We couldn't speak
each other's language, but we made friends through music.

Returning to the UK, she trained as an accountant, and for
several years worked in the corporate sector at senior management level.

I travelled the world business class, had share options, a
smart car, and was financially independent. There was huge
responsibility with it, and I learned how to manage large
teams across all corners of the world. I had climbed high
up the greasy pole, but whenever someone asked me what
I did, I was always embarrassed to say, 'I'm an accountant.'
I just didn't feel it was me. They owned me and the hours
were intense. I wasn't particularly happy or fulfilled.

Helen was playing in an orchestra that Mark Heron conducted, and as professor of conducting at the Royal Northern College of Music he would invite players to bolster the guinea-pig orchestra for his student conductors. This reignited the interest she'd had since her youth orchestra days. Blackpool Symphony Orchestra was looking for a conductor. She applied and got the job.

I was in front of musicians again. I realised I needed some training and after a few short courses, Mark suggested I took an Associate CPD year at the RNCM. This allowed me to observe on all the courses I felt would help me. My music degree at Cambridge gave me the academic tools required for a conductor, but I had no idea about conducting technique.

Helen gave up her 'day job' and decided to make her life in music. She started teaching with some conducting, and the balance shifted as she quickly became a much sought-after conductor in the county. Helen is a natural communicator, and her time in the corporate world has not been wasted.

I had years of training in leadership style – use of language, how to motivate and manage people who were sometimes much older and more experienced than me. In my old life I was known to be 'firm but fair', and I carry that through into conducting. In the business world it is utterly unacceptable to yell at your colleagues, so I wanted to get a proper training as a conductor. I'd noticed that some conductors of amateur orchestras would yell because they weren't properly in control, they didn't have the skills, and they saw it as the only way of getting what they wanted. That has changed in recent years, with so much better training available.

Like so many conductors of youth and amateur orchestras around the world, Helen is in the very heart of the community that gave her such a great musical start in life. She is returning that gift many times over.

Community

Every orchestra and opera company has a department dedicated to reaching out to the wider community, and of course there is much crossover with the rest of the organisation. The name for this department changes over the decades as does the message it hopes to convey to society – from 'education' to 'outreach' to 'learning and participation' to 'engagement, participation and learning'. Where do conductors fit into this? There's plenty of work for them here, especially early in a career, but I'd be lying if I said that this is an area that all conductors embrace. There are some fine conductors who are never engaged to conduct this genre of music, and while they respect the work, it's probably not where their strengths lie, and their schedule is so full already. But, sad to say, there is also some snobbery around it, which like all prejudice is born out of ignorance. Not so for Marin Alsop. Aside from her highly successful fourteen-year tenure as music director of the Baltimore Symphony Orchestra, she is the proud founding director of the Baltimore Symphony's OrchKids. This after-school programme provides music education to over 1,600 children.

> MARIN ALSOP: Playing an instrument was life-changing for me as a child and I believe everyone deserves access to this. I gained so many skills from playing in an orchestra; they weren't just musical, and it was also great fun. Who knows how many OrchKids will become professional musicians? That's not the point. I am so very proud of this work.

And the UK has some great examples of this too – Opera North and the Liverpool Philharmonic to name only a couple. The Benedetti Foundation is doing fantastic work, and like Marin, the violinist Nicola Benedetti is using her high-profile status to make a difference.

Bespoke Works

It was 13 August 2021, and gathered outside in the cloister of the Great Hall at the Dartington Festival were three choirs, two pianos, an electric guitar and two conductors, with the Brodsky String Quartet and a soprano soloist inside the hall. We were in the dress rehearsal for the world premiere of John

Barber's *Joy!* The sun was shining, which was certainly better than rain, but despite long discussions about where to place the choirs, none of us had thought about the problems of the sun in their eyes. No matter, they could cope with that. But quite amazingly we had also all forgotten about wind blowing the pages. I have a brilliant solution for this – wrapped around the music and the stand, elastic cotton both holds it down and allows you to page-turn. That is unless there's a big gust, which did happen a few times. It had been an anxious few hours. Half the artists in the festival had suddenly been forced to isolate, but by some fluke this had affected only one performer in *Joy!* – the soprano soloist Mary Bevan. Stepping into the breach came a very classy bursary student – Joanna Harries, who learned the music in a matter of hours.

This piece had been long in the planning and like so many projects had been due to be performed in August 2020 – a new commission by the festival's director Sara Mohr-Pietsch to celebrate Beethoven's 250th anniversary. The director and librettist Hazel Gould collaborated with John, running workshops with local groups in the community. Of course, with the events of 2020, the question of what brings us joy had changed, but most certainly joy was what we all wanted to celebrate, and John and Hazel had made something quite special. It is a wonderful thing to perform music that is written to reflect the present moment, and I spent a glorious week rehearsing this with the Festival Choir. They are all music readers and most sing in choirs at home, but for many this was the first time they had sung with others for over a year (and not down the Zoom line); however, with social-distancing rules strictly adhered to, they had to sit a couple of metres apart. This makes the experience quite isolating, though it has an unexpected benefit for a conductor. They can't have a little chat with their neighbour every time they stop singing, so it's a more focused rehearsal. It was great to have Hazel in the room, giving them some context, and taking them out onto the lawn and out of their comfort zone to do a little staging. That was until the day of the dress rehearsal when she got pinged and had to stay in her room.

Meanwhile singing specialist and choir leader Isabelle Adams was rehearsing and conducting a community choir and a children's choir – both with less to sing, but nonetheless vital to the piece. Isabelle belongs to a group of highly skilled musicians who can enable people of any age to sing confidently, healthily and with dramatic and musical intent. With tremendous energy, engagement and rehearsal skills, she can teach highly complex music to anyone. The written notation, which we classical musicians rely on so earnestly and – let's face it – snobbishly, is not necessary here. Isabelle will decode it for them and, with her honed musicianship and communication skills, will get people performing beyond anything they thought possible.

Joy! certainly wasn't easy but it had that ingredient essential to all good community works. It was singable, tuneful and with a rhythmic energy that was immediately appealing to singers, many of whom had very little experience in singing new music. By the time John arrived I was proud to show him something decent, and as the week progressed, he tweaked a few things that would help make it work for this group. Like most pandemic events, it had challenges that required artistic compromises, but in this case, there was something artistically satisfying about that. The compromises were part of the piece and the reason it was written. Yet its universal message allows it to stand on its own, and I am looking forward one day to performing it in a hall with everyone squashed together – and no wind to blow the music away.

This genre has emerged and grown exponentially during the past hundred years, particularly in the UK – works written to include young or non-professional performers, side by side with professionals. Some use universal stories from literature, mythology and religious culture, such as Benjamin Britten's *Noye's Fludde* (1958) or Jonathan Dove's *The Monster in the Maze* (2015). Some receive performances all over the world while others are bespoke works, devised for a specific community or culture, sometimes with unusual forces, and a storyline personal to that group. A conductor who is a team-player and facilitator is necessary here. They need to be a skilled communicator who can inspire and convey their intentions to a diverse group without resorting to patronising language, using musical jargon that baffles and intimidates, or simply losing their cool when things seem to unravel. One must trust that it will come together. That communication extends to those leaders on the ground doing all the hard work and preparation.

In July 2020 I was due to conduct Jonathan Dove's *The Monster in the Maze* at the Grange Festival in Hampshire. This opera was the brainchild of Simon Rattle and Simon Halsey and was jointly commissioned by Stiftfung Berliner Philharmoniker, London Symphony Orchestra and Festival International d'Art Lyrique d'Aix-en-Provence. It has enjoyed performances all over the world – always in the native language of that country. I accidentally ordered a version in Catalan from the publishers, which was rather annoying at the time. Telling the story of Theseus and the Minotaur, this opera has huge forces. There are three large choirs (children, teenagers and adults), three professional soloists and an actor. A large symphony orchestra accompanies them, normally divided into professional and youth – sitting side by side. There's also a brass band, entering the stage halfway through to represent the 'monster'.

At the end of 2019, Carl Clausen, the conductor of Hampshire Youth Orchestra, had started preparing them, meticulously planning and leading sectional and group rehearsals aiming towards the performances in mid-July. Some of those rehearsals were to include me, but the majority was to be done by Carl. Meanwhile another highly gifted singing specialist, Suzi Zumpe, was creating the three choirs from scratch. Very often such specialists will work closely with a stage director in workshops, so from the outset music and drama are combined. Tom Guthrie, who had directed the UK premiere, returned with a new production, and along with Suzi was busy recruiting in workshops way back in

2019. In February 2020 we recorded the voice of Stephen Fry to play the Minotaur. Installations and other clever stage effects were to give the impression of the monster who we could hear, but not see.

The conductor arrives much later in the proceedings. They may attend and conduct a few workshops, but their main role is to bring it all together in the last few weeks. Here I would have worked closely with the professional soloists, just as in a mainstream opera. In bigger rehearsals with a cast of mixed experience, a clear unambiguous conducting beat is important, but also an energy and dramatic drive. It is impossible to achieve any of this without the likes of Carl and Suzi. And, of course, most important of all is the composer. Not only had Jonathan written an exciting and perfectly formed work, but he is an expert in seamlessly writing for the non-professional and professional combined. Sadly for us another monster invaded all our lives in 2020 and it was not to be.

Back in 2012, I conducted a similar production: David Bedford's *The Wreck of the Titanic* at The Sands Centre, Carlisle. Artfully telling the famous story, this bespoke work for young musicians and professionals comprised huge forces – over four hundred children. The choirs and young players had been working with their teachers and music leaders all term. The instrumental tutors and I had been rehearsing the Cumbria Youth Orchestra intensively over the Easter holiday. We were staying at the Ullswater Outward Bound Trust Centre in the Lake District, and between rehearsals were engaged in wholesome outdoor activities. This was an inspired combination, since musicians tend to veer towards the indoors (dark gloomy practice rooms and the like), and of course it only helped with focus in rehearsals. I had a short time to put the whole thing together at The Sands Centre, and the teachers were very much part of that final performance – on stage with their groups, at times conducting them. This work was commissioned in collaboration with several UK county music hubs, enjoying performances around the country.

The desire to reach out and transport people to a happier place is at the core of many compositions, both for the listener and for the performer. Czech composer Hans Krása arranged the first performances of his opera *Brundibár* in the Theresienstadt concentration camp especially for the children there, most of whom eventually perished. I conducted this surprisingly joyous opera in a production by Frederic Wake-Walker with the Mahogany Opera Group. Performing with different children in different areas of England, it was fascinating to see how each time they brought something unique to the same production. However, the most poignant performance I witnessed was Rhian Hutchings's production at Welsh National Opera in 2019 conducted by their music director, Tomáš Hanus. Tomáš's mother was one of the few surviving members of the original Theresienstadt cast and, in an encore, all eight of his children joined him and the cast on stage to sing the finale – a celebratory song by the children who have defeated the evil organ grinder Brundibár.

There's no doubt that we are in a golden era today, yet this imaginative inclusive genre is nothing new. Benjamin Britten and Imogen Holst had been writing for mixed forces way back in the first half of the twentieth century. Aside from Jonathan, John and David, such leading composers as Errollyn Wallen, Roxanna Panufnik, and James MacMillan are part of a long list of fine composers who consider these compositions an essential part of their life's work. No box-ticking or dumbing down for them.

Training and Blurred Lines

For the best part of a decade, I have conducted productions with the Welsh National Youth Opera. Produced by Paula Scott in the WNO Participation and Learning Department this company blurs the lines between youth, community, training and giving opportunities to emerging professionals. Comprising singers, instrumentalists, stage managers, assistant conductors, directors and costume-makers from late teens to late twenties, it is led by a professional creative team and supported in all areas by the main WNO company. Both the 2013 production of Britten's *Paul Bunyan* (directed by Martin Constantine) and the 2016 production of Maxwell Davies's *Kommilitonen!* (directed by Polly Graham) won major national awards in the 'grown-up/professional' Best Opera category. In 2022 I conducted another triumphant production with them – Shostkovich's *Cheryomushki* with Daisy Evans directing.

What makes it so exciting is that none of us expects

anything less from the young company than we would from professionals, yet there is a subtle form of teaching and mentoring going on. In turn their commitment and lack of cynicism is infectious. The ethos is very much that of a company – a team. Inevitably there are bigger roles for the more advanced singers, many of whom are just starting in the profession, but they all are expected to take part in some chorus singing too. Any diva behaviour is firmly discouraged, and there is a warm supportive atmosphere in the company. This is something all the best opera productions should enjoy. Inevitably most of the cast are in full-time classical singing training, and these productions have been the starting point for some of the UK's leading opera singers. Every production includes people from non-classical backgrounds who are hoping to break into the alien and what can appear intimidating world of opera, and our track record for that is also good.

Site Specific

Another exciting ingredient is the site-specific production – taking the performance out of what can be the stifling environment of an opera house or concert hall. There are many more imaginative concert halls and theatres built these days, often in the round, and they can give a more inclusive feel. Sometimes the best thing is to go out into the community. Makeshift venues, often outside, are a good way of encouraging people back in. There are some wonderful initiatives in this area – the Street Orchestra Live, the Multi-Story Orchestra, the Nevis Ensemble and Manchester Collective, to name but a few. Many of them are founded by young visionary musicians, with conductors such as Holly Mathieson and Jon Hargreaves making a great impact alongside their more mainstream work.

The summer months are full of festivals, particularly opera. This area has grown so much in recent decades with some incredible purpose-built award-winning theatres springing up all over the country with all the 'mod cons', while still maintaining the outdoor performance vibe. What could be more idyllic than an opera performed outside to a group of picnickers? Nothing, if it doesn't rain. Instruments cannot get wet, for the obvious reason that they are extremely valuable and would be ruined, so a cover is always there for the orchestra. Despite my brilliant elastic-cotton trick, wind can still be a nightmare. I once conducted a whole Haydn opera with one hand, the other one holding down not just the pages, but the whole score and stand, which was threatening to fly away.

I think I probably win the prize for conducting in the most extreme temperatures ever. In 2018 I was asked by Stockholm's Folkoperan if I'd like to conduct excerpts of Puccini's *Turandot* as part of a sod-laying ceremony for Kiruna's new housing development. This most northern Swedish mining town was having to shift itself a few miles to keep the mine and the industry safe. Kiruna is in the Arctic Circle and the ceremony was to take place outside in February to an audience whose homes were to be moved to this new spot. When I received this email, after checking it wasn't 1 April, I said, 'Yes, please!' Two soloists and a répétiteur from Folkoperan performed with a local community choir. We all wore large cloaks from the Ice Hotel, and glass crowns over woolly hats. The set, beautifully lit, was the snow. In the rehearsal I wore two pairs of gloves and cut a tiny hole at the tip of the thumb and index finger, so I could turn the pages of the music. It was minus 28 degrees and after two minutes I was ready to cry, my hands hurt so much. One of the technical crew, taking pity on my foolishness, gave me some heavy-duty mittens. Painfully but quite quickly my hands thawed, I knew the music well, and realised I could easily conduct it from memory. Between the rehearsal and the performance, I asked for a small podium because not all the singers could see me. They found something that looked perfect, and it was only as I climbed onto it to conduct in the performance that I realised it was icy and very slippery. I managed to stay upright through sheer willpower, and perhaps the weight of the cloak helped keep me in place.

I just loved that experience, and not least because the audience seemed to love it, apparently not thinking it at all strange. As we made our way back to the minibus (as quickly as we could without falling over), a young man skilfully slid up to us. 'Thank you so much! That was amazing! I love opera but I've never heard an opera singer live before!' That's what makes my job worthwhile.

Part III

11: We Need to Talk about Breasts

Three Decades

'Surely not!' you say. I write this in the 2020s, not the 1970s, but I'm afraid we do need to talk about these appendages.

In 1979 Jane Glover was in the limelight – regularly on TV, she was one of the most well-known upcoming conductors in the country. This was her reason for moving to Glyndebourne Festival Opera as assistant conductor and chorus master:

> I wanted to work there because I needed to be a lowly cog in a mighty wheel, and to learn my trade, into which I had been thrust unprepared. I was attracting the wrong kind of attention, and there was this whole woman thing. Every time I stood up on the podium there were articles about me, about my shoes and my hair, and what the players thought of my breasts and all that nonsense.

How awful that Jane had to put up with that! How ridiculous that broadsheet papers, who would normally review the music, felt it important to review her appearance too. She was the trailblazer, the only woman doing the job, so indeed she did look different, but that doesn't need to be pointed out, and these weren't the fashion pages. It was the 1970s. Isn't it great that we no longer need put up with 'all that nonsense'?

Fast forward twenty years. It was the new millennium, and I was working as an assistant conductor and chorus master. Like Jane, I felt I needed time to develop. In the previous decade I had seen two talented conductors, Sian Edwards and Andrea Quinn, be thrust into the limelight in a not dissimilar way to Jane. They were young and sometimes given opportunities they weren't quite ready for. While they both survived this and went on to enjoy highly successful careers, it was a deeply challenging period for them. I was a few years younger and had watched and learned. To me it seemed that some of the people giving these opportunities didn't always believe women were capable of being conductors, and as soon as they struggled (which anyone would), it confirmed their belief that they weren't quite up to it. I didn't want to put myself in that position, and, late developer that I was, I felt I needed to take it slowly.

This was 2001 and a conductor I was working with told me why there are so few female conductors. I'm pretty sure I didn't ask for his views, but that wasn't going to stop him.

MAESTRO (*with no trace of irony*): Women can't conduct because their breasts get in the way.

I have thought of so many replies over the years – parts of his anatomy getting in the way of his powers of reason, etc.

At the time, I think I just laughed. He went on to argue that high levels of testosterone are needed to stand on the podium, to lead and inspire. I can't remember much more of what he said, as I soon stopped listening. I knew then that it was just a rude and silly comment, and there were plenty of male conductors I'd met who wholeheartedly disagreed with his viewpoint. The world had moved on from the 1970s. But it still got to me. If a well-respected and talented musician thinks that, then he's probably not the only one. I was at the start of my professional career, and this man was influential – someone who, if my work impressed him, had the power to open doors for me. He was telling me that my abilities were irrelevant simply because I had breasts, so I had to assume that these doors would remain closed. I searched for new doors. The good thing in my industry is that there are many doors, if you have the imagination and determination to look hard enough.

Well into the next decade, one evening in September 2013, I switched on my phone to see several missed calls from the BBC. I was intrigued, so I called them back. *The World Tonight* wanted to know what I thought of a well-known male conductor's alleged remarks that a cute girl on the podium is distracting to musicians. His comment had apparently been translated from English into Norwegian and back again and then taken out of context; he later retracted it. Marin Alsop was about to conduct the Last Night of the Proms, and suddenly the world outside the classical music bubble had noticed the distinct lack of women on the podium. They were wondering why this was – in 2013! I was near Millbank studio. I texted my mum and a close friend who worked in radio to tell them to turn on Radio 4, and thirty minutes later I was being interviewed by Robin Lustig – live down the line. After ignoring his first question ('Are you ever ogled at when you conduct?'), I started by challenging the assumption that it could be only men who'd be distracted by cuteness on the podium. Surely female or male cuteness could distract either men or women. I went on to explain that very few women were taking up conducting. Robin Lustig suggested that I might be a champion for young female conductors.

Until that day, I had lazily accepted that conducting was just something that women weren't drawn to, and that I was simply odd. I had experienced plenty of sexism, but I dared not admit it, even to myself. On the rare occasions when I ventured to suggest that perhaps certain behaviours towards me were a bit sexist, I was invariably told that I'd got it wrong, and that sexism was no longer an issue, or that I should just laugh at it. Deep down I knew they were wrong, but I learned there was nothing to be done, and it was best to button up and get on with it. Looking back, the thing that makes me most sad about those times is how accustomed I'd become to this sense of isolation. And because there were so few of us, I felt threatened by other women. We had all heard the comment of concert promotors, 'We've already had a female conductor this year. I don't think we need another for a while.' We were pitted against each other. I frequently gave myself a talking to on this – 'Don't be silly, this woman is an ally' – and on the very rare occasions when I met a fellow female conductor, we usually ended up having warm and interesting conversations, but we were guarded. Suddenly, in that very moment, I realised it simply wasn't good enough. Why not have more women doing it? Let's change it! Thank you, Mr Lustig, for planting that seed.

I've done many interviews since then, which were probably far more polished, but I will never forget that lightbulb moment. My mother – my harshest but fairest critic – was impressed. It was only after receiving approval from her and my radio friend that I admitted that earlier in the evening, not expecting any phone calls or interviews from the BBC, I had been out with friends and had drunk a whole bottle of wine. I should say that it is the only time in my whole career that I have touched a drop of alcohol before any kind of performance. It will never be repeated, but perhaps just that once it gave me the necessary clarity of thought.

It is 2020 – six years since I co-founded the Women Conductors programme, and twenty years since that comment by my conducting colleague. Many more women are training, winning competitions and forging very successful careers. We are out there doing well. Wonderful! Job done?

A masterclass for female conductors takes place with a major orchestra holding a well-respected international reputation. Most of the female participants have completed postgraduate study and have burgeoning careers. Feedback comes to the participants that a member of the orchestra has suggested some of them need to think a bit more carefully about what they wear on the podium.

The group is confused. They are all dressed smartly in trousers and shirts or polo-necks – the conductors' uniform. They ask for clarification. They are told it is because their breasts could be distracting, but this was considered a fair comment because it came from a woman.

I'm not the only person who is angry that this type of comment is seen by some as simply being helpful, and that it's perfectly reasonable for this message to be relayed. It's not helpful. Today, most musicians, male and female, young and old, would be utterly appalled by this story. Most of the time, what musicians care about in a conductor is if they can do the job well, in turn allow the musicians to do their job, are polite, respectful, and, one hopes, inspiring. Some of them might not believe it or think I have exaggerated these stories for comic effect. Sadly not, and even if these outdated sexist views are held by a tiny minority, they speak of a deeper issue that society still has with breasts and the female body, over forty years after Jane was having to contend with this.

Body Language

A conductor needs to open their arms wide. A symphony orchestra comprises about fifty to a hundred players, and they take up a lot of space. Your body must speak to every player in that group – especially the ones sitting on the edges

We Need to Talk about Breasts

who must listen extra hard because they are so far away from certain sections of the orchestra. This group is frequently ignored by inexperienced or unconfident conductors and gets thoroughly fed up. If a conductor's shoulders are turned in all the time, they will look as though they don't care, are self-indulgent, or unconfident.

I had first worked with Alma Sheehan at the Royal Welsh College of Music & Drama, where she teaches stagecraft to singers, and particularly admired her uncanny gift in kindly but shrewdly reading people, allowing her to give wise and tailored advice. Since working in opera for over twenty years, I've noticed that while singers are trained to project not just their voices but their whole physicality in performance, we instrumentalists give it little thought. We work very hard on what our bodies need to do in order to play the instrument, and that includes ensuring we are relaxed and comfortable, so we don't injure ourselves. However, we don't really worry about what we look like because music is an aural art form. But audiences can normally see us as well as hear us. Instrumentalists expect to look neat and tidy and sit up straight, but while singers remember to smile at the audience's applause (even when they feel miserable), instrumentalists might not think that's necessary. They're not being rude. They are just focused on other things. It's a pity, and I think more awareness and training should go into this performing element if we are to keep audiences coming to live concerts. So, when a talented instrumentalist wants to try conducting, they need to start exercising that acting muscle. Some find that easier than others. It's not about being fake or insincere, but rather about giving a more exaggerated version of yourself. Something that can be read by a large group.

Alma and I quickly noticed how reluctant women of all ages were to open their arms wide – basically revealing their chests to the world. The participants would try to open up and seemed to find it liberating. They could see, when watching each other, how much more confident and more like a conductor they looked when they did this. But after a few seconds of conducting, their shoulders would hunch in as if trying to hide or protect their chests from the world. And naturally this closed down their communication. 'Open up your shoulders!' was probably my most used phrase in those early days of teaching.

So, what exactly is going on here?

Conductors come in all shapes and sizes – male and female. Conducting is very physical, and our upper bodies must move freely, like dancers do, to be fully engaged in the music and communicate our ideas. We should always wear clothes that allow us to do that comfortably, and make sure that everything is securely in place. The orchestra needs to focus on a conductor's hands and face, so dangling earrings, shiny watches, busy patterned tops, etc., are inadvisable. But no conductor can entirely hide their shape, and nor should they.

Yet why does this 'distracting breasts' argument keep rearing its ugly head? What is it that makes breasts so unacceptable, funny or even shameful to some? If it is purely about sexual attraction or distraction, then the argument I gave in that *World Tonight* interview still stands, that this can work both ways. Men and women can be attracted to the male conductor's body too, but no one has ever suggested this might be a distraction, or a bad thing. When I'm conducting a ballet, I will have to look up from the pit at a tight-clad male dancer on stage, showing his stunning physique in all its glory, leaving little to the imagination. I need to make sure the tempo works for his dancing, so I look at his feet and sometimes his arms. That's my job. I don't get distracted.

Has history conditioned us to believe that breasts make women look less professional, less like a leader? If not sexual, then do they make women look a bit 'matronly' or 'mumsy'? Do we ever say 'dadsy'? Are we saying that only flat-chested women should be allowed on the podium? Or do those with larger chests need to wear a large sack?

We are making progress. I've noticed something wonderful evolving over the past six years. I run one-off workshops all over the UK and further afield, so I meet different women every time – hundreds of them aged sixteen upwards. In recent years, I rarely find I need to give the 'open up your shoulders!' encouragement. Perhaps at the start when they are feeling a bit nervous, but they quickly embrace it. It's familiar, and no longer scary for today's young women. That makes me very happy, but let's keep it that way and call out any time we hear these comments, because it won't take much for us to go backwards. If it is still considered acceptable to suggest breasts are distracting, then some of those newly empowered women will shrink right back into themselves. My advice to those who find breasts distracting is to ask themselves why this is, and not put the problem back to the conductor who cannot change their shape.

Dress

It's not just our breasts that get singled out for comment, even today. It is sad that I have to write about appearance, but this is not a superficial subject; it speaks deeply of our cultural attitudes to women. The iconic image of a conductor from way back in the nineteenth century is a man in tails. Still today this is the conductor's uniform, though often they are seen in smart black shirts and trousers. Male conductors' choices are simple, and I am most envious of them. I have had so many wardrobe conversations with my female colleagues, not because we are vain or shallow, but because we have all endured unkind or patronising comments about our appearances early in our careers, and reviews today do still sometimes include mention of the female conductor's clothes. I wonder if an overweight male conductor has ever been told to wear a slightly less tight-fitting shirt because his protruding belly is distracting – or even, come to that, his man-boobs. I doubt it. The problem is that the female alternatives to smart evening dress (tails, dinner jackets or lounge suits) are either a full-length ball gown with 'opera' gloves or a cocktail dress – the little black dress. These are not outfits designed for someone to leap around in. Some conductors can carry it off, but they're not something I'd ever want to wear on the podium. And I don't want to dress up like a man. It's fine if that's a look you're comfortable with, but for me personally it would feel as if I were saying that you must look like a man to do the job. I've found clothes that work for me and have had copies made when I can't buy replacements.

The interesting and exciting thing now is that as the image of a woman on the podium is becoming normalised, so too the variety of wardrobe increases. I like the confidence this is giving women to dress in what makes them feel comfortable. But debate as to what's considered acceptable continues.

TIANYI LU: It is much more complex for women. When I first started participating in masterclasses I tried to be as asexual as possible. I got told not to wear sleeves that hung down, and actually that was useful advice, because the extra movement they made was distracting, and I don't think that was sexist.

As women we can have more fun than men, and I certainly enjoy the process of putting on make-up before a concert. That peaceful moment in the dressing room.

TIANYI LU: I notice that when I put on make-up and 'beautify myself', it can make me feel more confident, and I don't see that's a distraction. Last year I was sick of the conducting clothes I'd been wearing, so I went shopping with some friends. They asked me, 'Why do you have to wear a jacket? Why not a sparkly dress?' I don't yet feel comfortable with a sparkly dress on the podium, but I suppose it's good to think outside your comfort zone a bit and it's also about context. I did a concert for Chinese New Year, and in the first half I wore a Chinese outfit, and more formal Western clothes in the second half.

EÍMEAR NOONE: The great thing about conducting at the Oscars was that it gave me the opportunity to put another woman on the stage. I called my friend the designer Claire Garvey and said, 'We're going to the Oscars!' There was no way I was wearing a black trouser suit on the red carpet – it was a gold dress for me.

Hair can be an issue if it covers a conductor's face and gets in the way of their eyes. My hairdresser says I'm the only person who ever studies the cut at the back when he holds the mirror behind me to check. That's what the audience sees. I always feel a bit sorry for male conductors in a theatre pit, where the view from the audience is the top of their head, and even with someone who seems to have a decent head of hair, the tell-tale signs of balding can't be hidden.

I think Simon Rattle's hair has got quite a bit of press over the years too, but it's never been suggested that his marvellous curly locks weaken his prowess on the podium. Quite the reverse, and there are several wild curly-haired male conductors out there doing extremely well. When interviewing Kalena Bovell, an American of African and Hispanic descent, I was appalled to hear that she had recently been told on a social media platform that she should straighten her hair and tie it back. Supporters on the platform quickly came to her defence, and eventually this same critic agreed that perhaps it was OK for 'pop concerts', but 'definitely not for Mozart or Beethoven'. Strange, when Beethoven himself had such a beautiful mane of curly hair. This was a double whammy of racism and sexism that Kalena had to endure. I was delighted to see her confidently ignoring that advice as she took to the podium for a thrilling BBC Proms debut in 2021.

WoCo

My goal since that BBC interview in 2013 has been to normalise the idea of women on the podium, so people would stop focusing on appearance, or lumping us together as one type of conductor. Just a few years before, one promoter had said to me, 'We tried a few women conductors in recent years, and it hadn't gone well, so we don't think they work with our orchestra.' It was clearly a numbers game. The more women stepping onto the podium, the less it becomes about their gender and the more it's simply about the music and whether they can do the job. There was a similar 1.4 per cent gender ratio around the world. A quick fix wasn't an option because, with the best will in the world, orchestras couldn't simply appoint women to these positions and shift that ratio.

There was only a tiny handful doing well, and another small group who might have been passed over or ignored for so long that they were behind their male counterparts in terms of work experience. I didn't want to be part of a lobbying organisation that demanded women be given positions they were not ready for. I could see how counterproductive and damaging that would be and, in any case, it would surely be seen as blatant self-promotion. Thus far, Marin Alsop was about the only person who had made any concrete effort to do something about it, having created the Taki Alsop Conducting Fellowship over ten years before. That was for women already on a training path and had more of a US focus at the time. I decided to stick to persuading talented young women who really wanted a career in classical music that conducting was at least an option to consider. No one could really argue that the tiny number of women applying to postgraduate conducting courses was acceptable.

At the time I was director of the opera course at Morley College – a south London adult education college with an illustrious musical history. The day after the BBC interview I went straight to the college's music director, the choral conductor Andrea Brown, whose predecessors include Gustav Holst and Michael Tippett. Within weeks we had cooked up an idea that, largely thanks to her fast-moving actions, gained Arts Council England funding. In March 2014 we ran the Women Conductors at Morley Pilot Programme – a three-day course for six participants. The year 2014 was a time when women seemed to be embracing feminism again. The Southbank Women of the World Festival was enjoying its third year. Our course was perfectly timed. It gained not inconsiderable interest from the press, not just in classical music and not just in the UK. We even made it into *Private Eye*, which was probably the only negative coverage we received. The article was full of factual inaccuracies, and Andrea batted it away with a masterful letter, which the magazine published, recommending that the anonymous journalist might benefit from a course in basic journalism at Morley College. The pilot course was quickly followed in 2015–16 with more ACE funding, allowing us to run sixteen weekend workshops.

Yet these were nerve-racking times. My initial plan was to target music students aged approximately sixteen to twenty-six. Calling on favours from friends and colleagues, we managed to persuade most of the UK music conservatoires and Oxford and Cambridge Universities to get on board. Our vision was to run weekend workshops around the country inviting all female music students (not just at those institutions) to apply. My instinct that young women were not seeing themselves as conductors was sadly more accurate than I had realised. Initially the uptake was poor, and I had many sleepless nights, fearing that this brilliant idea that so many people had invested in wasn't quite so brilliant if no one wanted to take part. Thanks to some clever PR work, and word of mouth from those who'd attended the first workshops, the numbers picked up very quickly and it started to become oversubscribed.

In Good Hands

One of our big success stories quite early on was Olivia Clarke, whose versatile talents gave her exactly the right credentials to become a conductor. An Oxford graduate, she had held an organ scholarship at Queen's College, and was studying for a master's in singing at the Royal Conservatoire Scotland. Alongside her obvious musical gifts, her singing training meant that she had no problem occupying the podium space and projecting her personality. I was delighted that within the year, after changing her second study from piano to conducting with Jessica Cottis, she was accepted onto a full-time master's course in Berlin. She recently held the Charles Mackerras Conducting Fellowship at English National Opera and is on a fast and well-deserved upward career trajectory. I suspect conducting might well have found her eventually, but I was glad to help her make the shift and decide to take that path.

A parallel group of women was contacting me. Women of all ages but not students were frustrated that I hadn't opened this opportunity up to them. I heard many stories of brilliant female musicians whose ambitions to become a conductor had been thwarted before they even began, whether through lack of encouragement or sometimes active discouragement from teachers: from the blunt and inaccurate 'That's not a job for a woman' to the downright offensive 'You're a very good musician, but you could never be a conductor because your breasts are too big.' (Yes, it's the breasts again.) How lucky that none of my teachers had said things like that to me in those early years of education and training!

So, Andrea and I had an excellent reason to create new workshops for this group, but I was reluctant to merge the two completely. Music students (most of whom are younger) have different issues to deal with as they prepare to launch themselves into the industry, and options for completely changing career direction are more vital and easier to navigate. I noticed for example that of the composers who conducted their own music, there were virtually no women except Shirley Thompson, the English composer of Jamaican descent who was breaking many stereotypes. By this stage I had honed a workshop based on my personal experience and training, and I felt reluctant to hand it over to anyone else. However, there was a handful of vastly experienced female conductors living or working in the UK, who had so much to offer these women. By the end of 2016 Jane Glover, Sian Edwards, Julia Jones, Andrea Quinn, Jessica Cottis, Rebecca Miller and Sarah Tenant-Flowers all delivered workshops – each focusing on one of their specialisms.

I needed to find a new home for this somewhat unwieldy programme, and Rosie Johnson and the Royal Philharmonic Society was suggested to me. Founded over two hundred years ago, the RPS has been championing music, classical musicians and composers ever since. The world has them to thank for Beethoven's Ninth Symphony. The much coveted RPS Awards are the BAFTAs of classical music. WoCo at the RPS grew in reputation and when in 2018 James Murphy took over from Rosie, I knew this relationship would continue. Formerly managing director of the Southbank

Sinfonia, James had been providing young players for my workshops since the pilot course. At the Association of British Orchestras Annual Conference in 2017 he had laid out, in no uncertain terms, the stark reality of the lack of female conductors not just in orchestras but also on management rosters. WoCo at the RPS continues to flourish today.

International

My reputation over the years led me to become involved in other programmes on three continents. In Sweden I discovered that Dirigent – Kultur i Väst had started something similar to WoCo at almost the same time and for the same reasons, and they invited me to teach. The Dallas Opera had started the Linda and Mitch Hart Institute for Women Conductors. This was for more advanced conductors, helping them get to that next stage and I spent a fascinating week working with the 2017 cohort. That year I was approached by Nigel Flegg and Ciara Cuffe at the National Concert Hall in Dublin and have enjoyed a remarkable collaboration there ever since as artistic director in two iterations of the Female Conductor Programme.

Probably the geographically and technologically most challenging programme for me has been with the Perth Symphony Orchestra; back in 2019 the CEO Bourby Webster invited me to help set up Women on the Podium with the orchestra's principal conductor Jessica Gethin. There are some very talented women, not just students, but many music teachers doing some awesome work in schools and youth orchestras in Perth. In just a few years, WOP has given confidence and helped develop careers for these women. I was in Australia for my second visit in early March 2020 and a few months later, Bourby emailed me: 'If we can get a small string ensemble together, and find a venue that allows us play, then how about you 'Zoom' in, and give a masterclass that way?' And that's what I did – appearing like 'Big Brother' on a screen as the conductors took to the podium. It worked very well, and we did more of this with Sian Edwards, Jessica Cottis and Jane Glover. The programme continues with a terrific team on the ground and with input from the other side of the world and sometimes even in person. We draw on conductors for discussion and teaching, which mostly works well, though chairing a Q&A with Sarah Ioannides, the music director of Symphony Tacoma in Washington State at 5 a.m. for me was fun but not something I'd like to repeat too often. With generous funding from the Perth business community, we are able to tailor the programme help women at many different stages and career trajectories.

Postgraduate and Beyond

As a conducting professor at the Royal Academy of Music, Sian Edwards had noticed a difference in standards between women and men applying for the master's in orchestral conducting. Since giving a masterclass on our WoCo pilot course, we'd had many discussions about this.

Quite rightly, she will take only the best applicants and was frustrated when she saw talented women who were not quite up to speed compared with their male counterparts. Mostly she felt the reasons were lack of confidence and not quite having sharp enough elbows to make sure they got those crucial experiences when undergraduates. The WoCo and NCH Dublin programmes were lighting the flame, but we needed to take this further. So, when the development department at RAM asked her to identify an area where it could help with diversity in conducting, she leapt at the chance. Generously funded by the Sorrell Foundation, in 2018 Sian began running courses – three or four weekends with instrumentalists and guest conductors. It is inspirational to be teaching alongside Sian on some of these weekends. I'm also proud to see women on these courses who had taken part in my early workshops and are developing into fine conductors. And, what's more, it worked. There are many more women getting places on postgraduate courses in this country, and in 2021 the two students accepted onto the MA course at the RAM were both women. As someone who struggled for so long to make that step, I am delighted that I can give the advice and expertise that I wish I'd had.

It's not just educational institutions that have backed us. There are substantial collaborations with The Royal Opera, The Royal Ballet and the Royal Northern Sinfonia. Other collaborations include the Hallé, the City of Birmingham Symphony Orchestra, Welsh National Opera, Royal Opera

House, Manchester Camerata, Southbank Sinfonia and the Dartington Summer School.

I am not really an advocate for single sex education, and I always encourage conductors to take part in courses with men as well. But as a small part of their journey into becoming a conductor, there is no doubt that this environment is needed for many women. Though the numbers continue to improve, they will probably be in the minority on most courses and finding their voice and identity can therefore be harder. The atmosphere on every workshop and masterclass I have taken part in has, without fail, been generous and collaborative. Friendships, networks and wider conversations of inclusivity have grown out of these events.

Just as conductors in their teens, twenties and thirties are benefiting from this, so too are older women who, having taken part in our advanced course, are better equipped to develop their careers. Alongside her other groups, Helen Harrison has made the move (with great ease) into working with professional ensembles. On the other side of the world Jen Winley, from a percussionist's career, through youth orchestra work, is now Assistant Conductor of the Western Australia Symphony Orchestra. Making that transition is unfairly seen as near impossible for men and women after a certain stage.

There is no doubt that as I write this the climate has changed dramatically. There are so many women doing well, not just at the training level, but much further into their careers. Women are winning international competitions, gaining assistantships with top orchestras and opera companies, and some women are being appointed as principal conductors and music directors to some of the major orchestras. It is and should be a slow process. This is wonderful. Is our work done? Not quite yet.

Work to be Done

It's great what you've done, Alice. But there's a tsunami of women conductors now, so be careful, it can go too far you know.

The problem is, some of the women clearly just got the job because they're a woman and look pretty on the album cover.

— is a fantastic conductor, but she's really difficult sometimes. Quite a tricky person to work with.

These are typical of the kind of comments I've received in recent years. For the record, I am not responsible for appointing women to these positions, nor have I lobbied on their behalf, so I really cannot take credit for that. But let's look at why these well-intentioned observations never fail to annoy me.

A tsunami is a very destructive thing, so that's an interesting word to choose – subconsciously or not. The gender ratio has massively increased, almost tripled in fact, but it is still hovering around 6 per cent, so I think a ripple is more accurate. Any new appointment of a woman tends to get extra media attention, so perhaps that skews the perception of the actual statistics. What on earth will happen when we reach double figures – 'a nuclear bomb of women conductors'?

I hope those figures in orchestral appointments will happen soon. When I took part in the Leeds Conductors Competition in 2002, there were two women out of 78 applicants. Hard to say precisely, but it would appear that about 20 per cent of the applications to competitions are from women these days, and they hold their own as the competitions progress, often becoming finalists and winners.

The second comment is harder to tackle. What is 'good' or 'bad' conducting? It is rare that members of an orchestra are unanimous in their opinions of any given conductor. Even when the majority really likes one conductor, another orchestra in another town or another country might form a completely different view of the very same person. Sometimes conductors might not be ready for the position they have been given, which can be damaging without the right support and understanding. There is no doubt that throughout the history of conducting, some less than talented male conductors have stood on that podium, but no one suggested their gender had anything to do with their supposed incompetence. As the journalist Jessica Duchen once remarked to me informally, 'Orchestras are always complaining about lousy male conductors, so why not have a few lousy female conductors too?'

As for being 'difficult' or 'tricky', there's plenty of research that points to female leaders in most professions being judged more harshly, and being labelled 'aggressive', where the same behaviour in men is seen as 'assertive'. The industry is rightly less accepting of badly behaved conductors, but a certain amount has been tolerated and is more likely to be forgiven in a man who 'gets results'. I recently had a conversation with someone who described one female conductor with years of experience as 'really good, but just too difficult to work with'. Within minutes, when talking about a male conductor with considerably less experience and expertise he said, 'Well, singers complained about him a lot, but I think he's really good, so he'll be coming back to us.' It does seem particularly unfair. When you consider how some women have had to fight hard to get where they are, don't they have more reason to be a little 'chippy' every so often?

Real Change

Quotas can be uncomfortable, even for those who consider them necessary for shifting the seemingly immovable status quo. I am sure, now that female conductors are being noticed, encouraged and supported in owning this podium space, that some men might find it harder to succeed. The truth is it was much easier for them before the likes of WoCo existed. Conducting is highly competitive yet largely an unregulated and unregulatable career, which sometimes makes it unfair. I can't apologise for trying to make it a little fairer by at least giving the other half of the population more of a chance.

I am very happy to see such wonderful female conductors coming through now and a giant shift in attitude has taken place. There's no doubt that the industry is trying hard to embrace this. It is becoming normal. No longer do I turn up to a rehearsal with a new group, baton in hand, scores under my arm, to be mistaken for a singer, instrumentalist or publisher. No longer, when I say I am music director for a production, am I asked, 'Great, but who's going to be conducting?' No longer am I metaphorically patted on the head and told, 'Oh, good for you! But isn't it conductress?'

Coda

I have just googled 'orchestral conductor' and clicked on 'images'. Perhaps this has to do with my algorithms, but the first photo is of a woman (Mirga Gražinytė-Tyla), followed by five men. In the first twenty images there are four women, and two conductors of black and ethnically diverse backgrounds. No conductor-shaped balloons in sight. We are making slow progress, and I am optimistic. Just as more women come into this wonderful profession and challenge the stereotype of the conductor, so it becomes more inclusive to all, and a larger variety of musical voices will begin to be heard. However, we are still talking about a narrow demographic, with class, race and income presenting huge barriers, and that's not just a female problem. The climate of inclusivity and society's expectations is shifting all the time, and I hope we can continue to change with it. The arguments are nuanced, therefore kind and generous conversation, imagination, vision and, above all, action are paramount if classical music is to thrive in the modern world.

Of the first hundred Google images in my search, there's only one of a conductor in rehearsal. The rest are all smartly dressed in black – either in a dramatic and energetic stance or still and meditative. There's an obvious reason for this. They are images that sell tickets. No one wants to see a poster of a sleep-deprived conductor, sitting at a desk, nursing a large cup of coffee with their head buried in a score. Rehearsal photos can look fantastic too, and unless a photographer can hide discreetly somewhere and snap away during a concert, or use a still from a video, the photos may well have been taken in rehearsal with the conductor dressing up for the occasion. It's not cheating, it's just being practical. The image of the smartly dressed charismatic performer is one the world expects to see.

Yet I have deliberately written very little about the public-facing performance. The reader can hear and see that for themselves. By telling the stories of modern conductors, I hope that this book has given an insight into what leads to the moment when they step onto the podium, lift their hands, and start the music.

Acknowledgements

In October 2020 I had taken a small window of travel opportunity and escaped to Stockholm's archipelago for a scene change. A surprise email appeared from Greg Morton, who at the time was a literary agent for WGM Atlantic. He asked if I'd ever considered writing a book. No, I had not.

He was imagining it more as a kind of memoir/professional reveal than a technical handbook. 2020 was surely a time when performing artists, having lost their *raison d'être*, were looking for temporary outlets for their creativity, not least to bat away fears that normal life might never return. I had been teaching on Zoom and reading books on conducting, but for several hours of every day, I was fully immersed in painting acrylics on canvas with varying degrees of success. Pictures of lockdown walks, favourite holidays from happier times, and even a few conductor portraits, helped me wait for life to return, and I was relishing the peace and satisfaction this gave me. However, Greg was persuasive, and I agreed to put down the paintbrushes, start writing and interviewing some of my favourite conductors who, like me, had time on their hands. Helped by a stupendous Baltic Sea view, some words, sentences, and a structure began to emerge. As I write this, I am back in the archipelago, grabbing just a few days' downtime between rehearsals. Life did resume, albeit haltingly for a while, and now is back to full speed. I am so grateful to Greg for spotting the moment and believing that I might be someone to take up the challenge, and for expertly guiding and encouraging me in those early months.

The book would be very slim indeed were it not for the conductors who so generously gave me their time and spoke so candidly and wisely. I would especially like to honour Bramwell Tovey who sadly died on 12 July 2022. He was one of the first conductors I thought to interview, and though I had only met him earlier that year, I knew he was just the kind of generous-hearted voice I wanted for the book – his informal manner belying a serious, deep-thinking musician. After a long, thought-provoking interview on Zoom, our time zones straddling the day, we both admitted to be wearing pyjama bottoms.

Thank you also to friends and family who have helped and encouraged me:

Zillah Watson and Hazel Gould for reading early drafts and their kind and helpful insights into creating a structure and narrative, and to friends and colleagues who read sample chapters.

Belinda Matthews at Faber for her kind encouragement and expert guidance throughout, and Jill Burrows and Joanna Harwood for patiently taking a novice writer through the editing process.

James Murphy, Robin Sheffield, and Camilla Carden for an inspiring office Christmas party where we finally landed on a title.

My big sister Jessica, who is the real writer in the family, but has been unstinting in her support of me throughout this process and my whole life.

Though they are not alive to read this, to my parents, who ensured music was part of everyday life, and who let our imaginations run free.

Index

Adam, Adolphe, Giselle, 219
Adams, Isabelle, 247
Aldeburgh, 226, 235
Alsop, Marin: biography details, ix;
    community work, 245–6; conducting
    teacher, 121–2; humour, 83; language
    and culture, 142–3; life-changing
    concerts, 44–5; on office jobs, 147;
    score preparation, 67, 228; speaking to
    audience, 86; training, 97–8; Women
    Conductors programme, 272; women
    conductors reception, 261
Andersson, Örjan, 189
Andriessen, Louis, 225
apprenticeships, 88, 159, 164–6
Aranovna, Anna, 101
Arnold, Malcolm, 199; English Country
    Dances, 199
Arts Council England (ACE), 272, 273
assistant conductors, 78–9, 94, 134–5,
    179, 185, 190
Association of British Orchestras, 276
Atkinson, Sandra, 156–7
audiences, 1–5, 86
auditions, 95, 103, 137, 147
Auld, John, 199

Bach, Johann Sebastian, 23, 48, 89, 242
Baker, Richard, ix, 52, 56, 193, 225–6,
    227, 230
ballet, 195–221; ballet class, 209–11; ballet
    pianists, 208–9; bridge between two
    worlds, 219–21; language, 202–5; male
    dancer body, 267; notation, 205–6;
    overview, 195–202; rehearsals, 206–8;
    repertoire, 217–19; Russian language,
    107; Seletskaja as exception, 211–17
Baltimore Symphony Orchestra, 245

Barber, John, 245; Joy! 246, 247–8
Barbirolli, John, 83
Barenboim, Daniel, 166
Barlow, Stephen, 5
bar numbers, 63, 234–5
Barry, Gerald, 226
the basics: hands and baton, 30–41; the
    baton, 38–41; beating time, 32–5;
    conducting Charades, 37–8; expression,
    35; how to start, 31–2; mini-guide,
    31–8; sound, 36–7; volume, 35; waving,
    30–1
baton technique, 38–41, 68, 72, 108–9,
    136
BBC Concert Orchestra (BBCCO), 1
BBC Radio, 5, 21, 161, 261–3, 271–2
BBC Schools, 36
BBC Symphony Orchestra, 84
beating time, 32–5, 110
Beckett, Gwendoline, 44
Bedford, David, The Wreck of the Titanic,
    250–1
Beecham, Thomas, 83
Beethoven, Ludwig van, 12, 64, 89, 246,
    271; Fifth Symphony, 10–11; Ninth
    Symphony, 275
bel canto, 219
Belfast Ensemble, 224
Bellini, Vincenzo, Norma, 152, 156, 169,
    219
The Benedetti Foundation, 245
Benesh Movement Notation (BMN), 205
Berklee College of Music, 213
Bernstein, Leonard, 44, 76, 86, 127
Bevan, Mary, 246
Birmingham Royal Ballet, 199, 200, 217
Bizet, Georges, Carmen, 189, 190
Blackpool Symphony Orchestra, 240, 243

In Good Hands

blocking, 173
Bob, 226–7
body language, 113, 264–8
Borås Symphony Orchestra, 238–9
Boult, Sir Adrian, 44, 84
Bovell, Kalena, ix, 53–4, 132
Brabbins, Martyn, 128
breasts, 259, 260, 261, 264, 266, 267–8, 274
breathing, 28, 31, 32, 37, 72
Britten, Benjamin, 36, 140, 225, 235, 252; Noye's Fludde, 51, 248; Paul Bunyan, 252; The Rape of Lucretia, 141; War Requiem, 21
Brodsky String Quartet, 245
Brown, Andrea, 272, 273, 275
bullying, 83, 123, 124, 132, 133
Bychkov, Semyon, 108

Calgary Opera, 156
Callas, Maria, 159
Cambridge University, 241–2, 243, 273
careers, 126–47; competitions, 128–34; different paths, 134–6; the label of conductor, 126–8; language and culture, 139–44; marketing skills, 136–9; office jobs, 145–7; titles, 144–5
Carmen Moves, 189
Charles Mackerras Conducting Fellowship, 274
children, 36, 45, 47, 161, 245, 247, 251
choirs, 21–2, 24–5, 30, 49, 153–4, 247
choreography, 205–6, 207, 217
choruses, 61, 171–2, 207
'circle', 110, 111, 112, 113
City of Birmingham Symphony Orchestra, 278
Clarke, Olivia, ix, 54, 57, 80, 132, 274
Clausen, Carl, 249, 250
Cleall, Charles, 44
Clergy Orphan Corporation, 19, 23
'click', 110, 111
click tracks, 229–30, 233
clothing, 259, 264, 266, 268–71, 284–5
competitions, 128–34, 147, 279, 281
composers, 217, 222–3, 228, 233–6
composition, 222, 225–6, 231

conducting: ballet, 195–221; the basics: hands and baton, 30–41; careers, 126–47; lighting the fire, 42–59; new music, 222–36; opera, 151–94; overviews, 1–14, 284–5; preparation to performance, 60–87; reaching out, 237–55; the start, 17–29; training, 88–125; women conductors reception, 259–83
conservatoires, 5, 94–5, 99, 115, 273
Constantine, Martin, 252
contemporary music see new music
Cornelius, Gerry, 102
Cottis, Jessica, 274, 275, 277
Coventry Cathedral, 153
Covid-19 pandemic, 8, 121, 246–7, 248, 250
Cuffe, Ciara, 276
Cumbria Youth Orchestra, 250
Cummings, Laurence, ix–x, 51–2, 192–3
Currentzis, Teodor, 108

Dallas Opera, 276
Danby, Nicholas, 23
dance notation, 205–6
Dartington Festival, 235, 245, 279
Davis, Sir Colin, 146
Dingle, Susie, 102
diversity, 6, 14, 284
Dove, Jonathan, 223, 224; Gaspard's Foxtrot, 223, 224; The Monster in the Maze, 248–50
downbeats, 33
Downes, Edward, 159, 160
dress, 268–71, 284–5
dress rehearsals, 188, 220
Drummond, David, 94
dub stage, 232
Duchen, Jessica, 281
dynamics, 65–6

Edwards, Sian: biography details, x; on brass bands, 238; Cambridge University Chamber Orchestra, 242; competitions, 129–30; conductor training, 8, 120–1, 122–3; label of conductor, 126–7; making of conductors, 50–1, 55–6;

Musin and Russia, 99–101, 118–19; rehearsals, 81–2; score preparation, 64; St Petersburg school, 116; training course, 95–6; Women Conductors programme, 275; women conductors reception, 260; WOP masterclasses, 277

Eggar, Katherine, Idyll, 234

Elder, Mark, 159, 160

Elgar, Edward, 43; Enigma Variations, 44, 217; 'Nimrod', 4

Ellis, Philip, 200, 202

English National Opera, 54, 154, 274

English Opera Group, 36

Estonia, 52, 213, 215

Estonian National Ballet, 211, 212

European Chamber Opera, 94

Evans, Daisy, 252

expression, 35

Faking It, 60

Fauré, Gabriel, Requiem, 27, 29

female body, 264–8

female composers, 233–6, 275

Female Conductor Programme (Dublin), 138, 276, 278

female conductors see women conductors

La Fille mal gardée (ballet), 195, 214, 218

film and media music, 4, 230–3

Fitkin, Graham, 4, 217

Flegg, Nigel, 276

foldback microphones, 160, 185

Folkoperan, Stockholm, 189, 254–5

Fowke, Philip, 42

French language, 105, 139, 140, 209

Fry, Stephen, 250

gaming music, 231, 233

Garton, Graham, 22, 58–9

Garvey, Claire, 270

gender ratio of conductors, 6, 59, 271, 280

Gergiev, Valery, 108, 114, 119

German language, 139–40, 140, 142

Gethin, Jessica, 276

Glass, Philip, Satyagraha., 191

Glassberg, Ben, x, 45, 54–5, 81, 132

glasses, 63

Glover, Jane: biography details, x;

language and culture, 142; life-changing concerts, 43; making of conductors, 50; opera apprenticeships, 164; rehearsals, 77, 79, 85; training, 97; university training, 90–1, 242; Women Conductors programme, 275; women conductors reception, 259, 260; WOP masterclasses, 277

Glyndebourne, 79, 151, 154, 164, 194, 195, 259

Gothenburg Opera, 159, 171, 238

Gould, Hazel, 246, 247

Graham, Polly, 190, 252, 283

Grange Festival, 249

Grant Thornton Ireland, 138

Gražinytė-Tyla, Mirga, 284

guest conductors, 139, 144, 145, 202

Guido Cantelli Conducting Competition, 131

Guildhall School of Music & Drama, 5, 97

Guthrie, Tom, 249

Guy's & St Thomas's Hospital, 93

hair, 259, 270–1

Haitink, Bernard, 79, 164, 197, 217

Halsey, Simon, 249

Hampshire Youth Orchestra, 249

Handel, George Frideric, Messiah, 21

hands see the basics: hands and baton

Hanus, Tomáš, 251

Hargreaves, Joe, 254

Harries, Joanna, 246

Harrison, Helen, x, 53, 57, 240–4, 279

Haydn, Joseph, 254; La fedeltà premiata, 5; 'Nelson' Mass, 29

Hérold, Ferdinand, 218

Heron, Mark, 243

Hertel, Peter, 218

Heyward, Jonathon, x, 55, 57–8, 80–1, 132

Hinnells, Duncan, 155

Holst, Gustav, 235, 272

Holst, Imogen, 235, 252

humour, 83–5, 234–5

Hutchings, Rhian, 251

intonation, 69, 240

In Good Hands

Ionnides, Sarah, 277
Italian language, 34, 139–40, 158
Italian opera, 158, 180, 219

Jacobs, Paul, 138
Jansons, Arvid, 100
Jansons, Mariss, 100
Järvi, Neeme, 99
Järvi, Paavo, 216
jazz, 3
Johnson, Rosie, 275
Jonathan (child conductor), 10–11
Jones, Julia, 275
Jordan, Philippe, 45
J. P. Guivier and Co., 40
Jubilee Hall, Calgary, 152
Juilliard School, 75, 97

Kane, Sarah, 230
King's College, Cambridge, 22
Kirov, 196
Kiruna, Sweden, 254
Knussen, Oliver, 226–7
Korchmar, Leonid, 119–20, 124
Krása, Hans, Brundibár, 251

Lanchbery, John, 218
languages, 139–44, 158, 202–5
Leeds Conductors Competition, 281
Leningrad Conservatoire, 99, 108
Leonhardt, Gustav, 197
libretto, 158, 167–8
Liceu, Barcelona, 165
Lichfield Cathedral, 52, 225
Linbury Theatre, 217
Linda and Mitch Hart Institute for
    Women Conductors, 276
Liverpool Philharmonic, 245
London Festival Ballet, 122
London Mozart Players, 235–6
London Philharmonic Choir, 154
London Philharmonic Orchestra, 42, 43,
    44
Lu, Tianyi, xi, 53, 58, 80, 125, 131, 132,
    269–70
Lully, Jean-Baptiste, 39–40
Lustig, Robin, 262, 263

Lyric Opera, Chicago, 166

Maazel, Lorin, 74, 76, 154
MacMillan, James, 252
MacMillan, Kenneth, Las Hermanas,
    198–9
Mahler, Gustav, 45; Das Lied von der
    Erde, 217
Mahogany Opera Group, 251
male composers, 233
male conductors: comments on
    competence, 281–2; dress and
    appearance, 268; hair, 270; master's
    degrees, 277; networking, 135; office
    jobs, 147; views on women conductors,
    260–1
Malko, Nikolai, 108
Manchester Camerata, 279
Manchester Collective, 254
Mariinsky Theatre, 119, 141, 196
marketing, 136–9
marking, 177–8, 188
masterclasses, 120, 123–5, 263, 269, 277
master's degrees, 89, 95–6, 215, 242,
    277–8
Masur, Kurt, 74, 76
Mathieson, Holly, 254
Matthews, Colin, 235
Mawby, Colin, 231
Maxwell Davies, Peter, Kommilitonen!
    189–90, 252
Mayhew, James, 223
McDowall, Cecilia, Off the Ground,
    235–6
Memphis Symphony Orchestra, 132
metronome markings, 34
Metropolitan Opera, 77
Miller, Rebecca, 275
Minkus, Ludwig, Don Quixote, 218
Mitchell, Conor, 224–5
Mohr-Pietsch, Sara, 246
Morley College, 7, 272, 273
Mozart, Wolfgang Amadeus, 45, 64, 89,
    165, 192, 271; C minor Mass, 29;
    Don Giovanni, 79; Le nozze di Figaro,
    90; 'Paris' Symphony, 1, 2, 3; 'Prague'
    Symphony, 56; Die Zauberflöte, 77, 94

Index

Multi-Story Orchestra, 254
Murphy, James, 275
musical notation, 205, 247
music directors, 144–6, 156–7, 171, 175, 178–9, 183–4
music education, 36, 47–8, 222, 244, 245
music theory, 34
Musin, Ilya Alexandrovich, 12, 98–108, 109, 110–19, 121, 124–5, 235

National Ballet of Canada, 211, 216
National Chamber Choir of Scotland, 231
National Children's Wind Orchestra of Great Britain, 45, 55
National Concert Hall (NCH), Dublin, 8, 121, 138, 276, 277–8
National Youth Orchestra, 238
nerves, 7, 28–9, 74, 75–8, 79, 81
networking, 135, 137, 138
Nevis Ensemble, 254
new music, 222–36; composers, 222–3; female composers, 233–6; film and media, 230–3; premieres, 223–5; score preparation, 227–9; specialists, 225–7; synchronisation, 229–30
New Works, 217
New York City Opera, 165
New York Philharmonic, 74–6
Nielsen, Inge, 165
Noone, Eímear, xi, 51, 57, 230–1, 232, 270
notation, 205–6, 247

office jobs, 145–7
offstage music, 185–7
opera, 151–94; apprenticeships, 164–6; finale, 187–8; the future, 194; language and culture, 139–40, 142; offstage music, 185–7; onstage rehearsals, 182–5; the orchestra, 179–82; out of the pit, 188–90; overview, 151–2; performances, 190–1; pre-rehearsal, 166–7; prompting, 157–64; rehearsals, 155–7, 170–3; score preparation, 167–70; seventeenth to twenty-first century, 192–3; singing, 153–5; stage directors, 173–9
Opera North, 245

Orchestra Unwrapped, 4
OrchKids, 245
organ playing, 31, 42–3, 61, 90, 92
organ scholarships, 23, 24–6
Oundle International Organ Week, 23
outdoor performances, 254
Oxford Music Group, 56
Oxford University, 7, 11, 23–9, 89–91, 225, 273

Panufnik, Roxanna, 252
Pappano, Antonio: biography details, xi; humour, 84; label of conductor, 127; language and culture, 144; making of conductors, 48–9; opera, 164–6, 170, 175, 180–1, 192; on performance, 85; rehearsals, 72, 77; score preparation, 67–8, 228
Peabody Institute, 97
pencils, 66, 168, 181
performance, 85–7
performances, repeat, 190–1
peripheral vision, 35, 63, 178
personality of conductor, 12
Perth Symphony Orchestra, 276
Petipa, Marius, 196, 218
Philharmonia Chorus, 154
Philharmonia Orchestra, 224
pianists, ballet, 207, 208–9
piano dress rehearsals, 220
pit, 188–9
Pochin, Juliette, 234
portamento, 204
postgraduate studies, 7, 89, 94–8, 277–80
precision, 109, 110
premieres, 223–5, 227
preparation to performance, 60–87; conductor behaviour and nerves, 73–82; humour, 83–5; overview, 60–1; performance, 85–7; rehearsals, 68–73; score preparation, 61–8
pre-rehearsal, 166–7
Prokofiev, Sergei, 217; Peter and the Wolf, 223, 224; Romeo and Juliet, 196
prompting, 157–64
Proms, 43, 261, 271
proscenium stage, 188

In Good Hands

Puccini, Giacomo, 72, 254; La Bohème, 165; Gianni Schicchi, 73; Turandot, 191, 254
'punches', 233
Puttick, Gladys, 49

Quinn, Andrea, 94, 260, 275

Ralph Vaughan Williams Trust, 235
Rattle, Simon, 127, 249, 270
Ravel, Maurice, 73
reaching out, 237–55; bespoke works, 245–52; community, 244–5; musician for life, 237–44; site-specific production, 253–5; training and blurred lines, 252–3
recitative, 172, 175
recordings, 10, 65, 137, 169, 205, 207, 209, 227, 232
Red House, Aldeburgh, 235
rehearsals: ballet, 206–8; opera, 5–6, 155, 170–3, 182–4; overview, 68–73; photographs, 285–6; pre-rehearsal, 166–7; warm-ups, 36
repeat performances, 190–1, 209
répétiteurs, 156–7, 165, 175, 179, 182, 185, 209
Rimsky-Korsakov, Nikolai, Capriccio Espagnol, 117
Robinson, Peter, 187
Rossini, Gioachino, Il barbiere di Siviglia, 192
Royal Academy of Music (RAM), 55, 95–6, 99, 122, 277, 278
The Royal Ballet, 196, 198, 199, 217, 278
Royal College of Music, 23, 93
Royal Danish Ballet, 142
Royal Northern College of Music (RNCM), 99, 104, 243
Royal Northern Sinfonia, 134, 240, 278
Royal Opera House (ROH), 54, 77, 157, 159, 162–4, 186, 217, 220, 278–9
Royal Philharmonic Orchestra, 102
Royal Philharmonic Society (RPS), 7, 134, 235, 275–6
Royal Scottish National Orchestra (RSNO), 223
Royal Welsh College of Music & Drama, 174, 265
Russia, 79, 98–108, 111, 114, 116–17, 120, 126, 127
Russian language, 105–7, 139, 140, 141

Sadler's Wells Royal Ballet, 198, 199, 219
Salvation Army, 49–50
Sargent, Malcolm, 83
Scharff, Christina, Equality and Diversity in the Classical Music Profession, 6
score preparation, 61–8, 167–70, 227–9
Scott, Paula, 252
Scottish Ensemble, Goldberg Variations, 211
Seletskaja, Maria, xi, 52–3, 211–16, 220–1
Service, Tom, 2, 3
Shchedrin, Rodion, 189
Sheehan, Alma, 7, 265, 266
Shostakovich, Dmitri, 57, 117; Cheryomushki, 252
sight-reading, 22, 68, 154
singing, 47, 71, 153–5, 181, 210
Sir Georg Solti International Conductors' Competition, 131
Sitzprobe (seated rehearsal), 182
Slorach, Ellie, 234
Smyth, Ethel, March of the Women, 234
Soanes, Zeb, 223
Society of Women Musicians, 234
solfège (ear training), 213
Sorrell Foundation, 278
sound, 36–7
Southbank Sinfonia, 220, 236, 275–6
Soviet Union, 212–13
stage-and-orchestra (S&O) rehearsals, 183–4, 188, 206
stage-and-piano (S&P) rehearsals, 182–3, 206, 220
stage directors, 173–9
staves, 61, 205–6
Sternfield, Frederick, 91
St Hugh's College, Oxford, 24–7, 27, 90
St Margaret's School, Bushey, 19–23
St Petersburg, 100, 102–3, 106, 124, 195, 221
St Petersburg school, 108, 110–20, 215
Stratford, Stuart, 103, 104

Index

Stravinsky, Igor, 217; Firebird, 204; Le Sacre du printemps, 196; The Rake's Progress, 193
'streamers', 233
Streatfeild, Noel, Ballet Shoes, 195
Street Orchestra Live, 254
Stuttgart Ballet, 214
surtitles, 158
Sweden, 167, 238–9, 254–5, 276
Swedish language, 140–1, 142, 158
synchronisation, 229–30, 232–3
Syrus, David, 159

Tabakova, Dobrinka, 4
Taki Alsop Conducting Fellowship, 143, 272
tap dance, 229
Tchaikovsky, Pyotr Ilyich: Capriccio Italien, 117; Nutcracker Suite, 118, 196, 212; Piano Concerto No. 1, 42, 43; Serenade for Strings, 217; Sixth Symphony (Pathétique), 3, 118, 119; Swan Lake, 196, 200, 202
teaching, 120–3
technical rehearsals, 182–3, 206
Temirikanov, Yuri, 108
tempo, 34, 210, 215, 216, 219
Tenant-Flowers, Sarah, 275
Theresienstadt concentration camp, 251
Thompson, Shirley, 275
Thomson, Neil, 93
Three Choirs Festival, 224
Tianyi Lu, xi, 53, 58, 80, 125, 131, 132, 269–70
time, beating, 32–5
time signatures, 33
Tippett, Michael, 272
Todd, Ray, 46
Toscanini, Arturo, 84
Tovey, Bramwell, xi, 49–50, 69–70, 74–6, 82, 83–4, 122, 125, 156–7
training, 88–125; conducting teacher, 120–3; London, 91–4; masterclasses, 123–5; Musin and Russia, 98–108; Musin technique, 108–9; overview of routes, 88; postgraduate studies, 94–8; St Petersburg school of conducting,
110–20; university, 89–91
transposing instruments, 64–5
Trinity College Dublin, 231
Trinity College of Music, London, 17, 49

University of California at Los Angeles, 231
university training, 7, 23–9, 89–91
upbeats, 37

Vaganova Ballet Academy, 221
Varah, Chad, 94
Venables, Philip, 4.48 Psychosis, 230
Verdi, Giuseppe: Aida, 62; La Traviata, 151, 219; Requiem, 46; Rigoletto, 170
Verrilli, Norma, 48
video footage, 73, 97, 121, 130, 137, 169, 205
volume, 35

Wake-Walker, Frederic, 251
Wallen, Carolyn, 252
Wand, Günter, 154
warm-ups, 36
Warnock, Mary, 50
Warrack, Dr John, 27, 89–90, 155
Watford Philharmonic Society, 46–7
Watford Town Hall, 42, 43, 47
Watkins, Jonathan, 217
waving, 30–1
Webster, Bourby, 276, 277
Welsh National Opera (WNO), 190, 251, 252, 278
Willcocks, David, 154
Williams Fairey Engineering Brass Band, Stockport, 238
Winley, Jen, 279
women composers, 233–6, 275
women conductors: body language, 264–8; comments on competence, 281–2; competitions, 134; conductors' workshops, 6–8; dress, 268–71; gender ratio of conductors, 59; images of, 284; international programmes, 276–7; Musin and Russia, 114–15; networking, 135; numbers of, 7; postgraduate studies and beyond, 277–80; real change, 282–

3; role models, 23, 79; stage directors, 174; Taki Alsop Conducting Fellowship, 143; three decades overview, 259–64; Women Conductors programme, 271–6; work to be done, 280–2

Women Conductors at Morley Pilot Programme, 272

Women Conductors programme (WoCo), 6–8, 120, 134, 234–5, 263, 271–8, 282

Women on the Podium (WOP), 276–7

Woolrich, John, 226

Wordsworth, Barry: ballet, 196, 197–9, 203, 204, 207–8, 210, 217, 218, 219–20; biography details, xi–xii; label of conductor, 127; on life-changing concerts, 44; making of conductors, 49; on office jobs, 146–7; rehearsals, 72; on Toscanini, 84

workshops, 6–8, 11–12, 36, 267, 273, 275

The World Tonight, 261, 267

Wright, Sir Peter, 199

wunderkind conductors, 127

Wyndham Chamber Orchestra, 92

youth orchestras, 47, 50, 52, 239–40, 244, 250

Zharasov, Nurlan, 101

Zumpe, Suzi, 249, 250